MY FIFTY YEAR NURSING JOURNEY

Why On Earth Would Anyone Want To Be A Nurse?

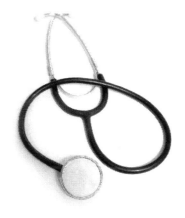

Barbara Ann Burke, NA, LVN, ADN, BSN, MSN

authorHOUSE®

1663 Liberty Drive
Bloomington, IN 47403
www.authorhouse.com
Phone: 1-800-839-8640

Published by AuthorHouse 6/21/2013

ISBN: 978-1-4817-6600-5 (sc)
ISBN: 978-1-4817-6599-2 (hc)
ISBN: 978-1-4817-6601-2 (e)

Library of Congress Control Number: 2013911080

Any people depicted in stock imagery provided by Thinkstock are models, and such images are being used for illustrative purposes only.
Certain stock imagery © *Thinkstock.*

This book is dedicated to my FAMILY...

To my children, who have been with me throughout most of my Nursing career and had to endure the process. You ate many Thanksgiving and Christmas meals in hospital cafeterias, celebrated birthday parties on days other than your actual birthdays due to my work schedules, and waited for me to pick you up from somewhere.... usually late rather than on time. You have fetched beverages and snacks during many study sessions in a living room full of Nursing students who were studying for exams and writing healthcare plans for tomorrow's clinicals. You also have sat through, in the rear of big college classrooms and lecture halls, many uninteresting lectures and classes I had to attend, having no available babysitter for you. Finally, for attending several crowded Nursing graduation ceremonies, at all ages, that lasted for hours in hot, noisy college auditoriums or convention centers.

To my first husband who briefly endured some of these same things, but MOSTLY to my current husband who, unable to use your own VA-awarded educational benefits, generously transferred them to me. This provided money to pay for both my Bachelor's and Master's degrees in Nursing.

More than anything else, you understood the importance of my career dreams and undying love for Nursing. You mutually respected and encouraged me toward my achievement of this final educational and career goal.

You were my test audience so many nights as you suffered silently while I read paper after boring paper to you. I was discussing topics you could care less about such as Healthcare Budget & Finance, Medical Ethics, and Algebraic equation solving. Then there was that final work of art, the Graduate School Thesis I worked so hard on day and night, on vacations and weekend campouts, for so long. It must have been the happiest last day of MY educational journey for YOU! Just to know that you would no longer have to hear me anguishing and wailing about how to determine the "variables between traditional Nursing education in the classroom and non-traditional Nursing educational methods of today online!" We did it!!! It was finalized in late 1999 and my years of continuing Nursing education are finally and forever over. Grad School....checked off and done!

AMEN!!

You are ALL my heroes and I know I have bored you all to tears so many times, but thank you for being there! I could NOT have done it without your love and support! It means so much to me to know that you were all beside me all the way. I only hope that I have made you all proud!

Thank You!!

WHAT IS A NURSE????

CHAPTER 1

Florence Nightingale expressed often that Nursing is an art. I believe this with all my heart and soul. What is a real Nurse? The true Nursing spirit is something which we nurture within our own soul and mind, put out there for the good, and hopefully, patients reap the benefits. It is who we are and what we do. It cannot be experienced casually and it IS who we are. Nursing is our life, and it defines us.

Nursing....so many aspire to it while others embrace it as a life. It is the ultimate, in my mind, of one of the most highly respected and chosen professions throughout the ages of mankind. It has been around for centuries as a, more or less, natural task undertaken by motherly women, and some caring men; anyone with an internal desire to physically and emotionally care for others. It should never be entered into lightly, not unlike marriage or parenthood. Nursing is serious business!

Some say Nursing is a calling and some say it is an inborn gift. If one can blend a natural desire to care for others with a long, demanding, and torturous education and training process, with a strong stomach, the ability to work any and all, odd-hour shifts alongside a variety of all personalities, one can become a successful Nurse. It is not to be underestimated by any means. If one is truly a dedicated Nurse, it draws daily and unmercifully upon social life, marriage, family time, sleep, emotions, and health. It consumes one in the lengthy mandatory Nurse training programs. It causes a metamorphosis that either moves one to a higher level in Nursing expertise, or leaves them well behind, along with the dreams of that naïve but well-intended person.

Many "used-up" Nurses are found in boutiques or business offices, as well as a multitude of other jobs, simply because they have tossed in the towel of Nursing due to an equal multitude of reasons. Nursing "Burn-out" is well known as the arch-nemesis of the Nurse, and is a reality. I have experienced it more than once and observed it in many of my fellow Nurses, with most of us having experienced it several times throughout our Nursing careers. Exhaustion, frustration, and concerns related to what Nursing has evolved into over the past few decades have taken their toll on Nurses of all ages and specialties. Long shifts, heavy patient loads, and lack of compassion within the systems, with loss of precious family time contribute to this meltdown. Some simply cannot give anymore of themselves or sacrifice any more personal or family relationships to their chosen career. Others become disillusioned with what Nursing has become in our modern money and technology-driven healthcare systems.

Even more Nurses fear that many current diseases are so highly terminal, and transmittable, they choose a less potentially deadly path for a career. Diseases today have morphed into something much more frightening than ever imagined. Medical dangers lurk out there in patient-care areas formerly thought to be safe. Litigiousness and malpractice are real dangers to Nurses daily. It appears today, for some, to just not be worth it!

Most often, however, it is based upon the fact that no one is taking care of the caretaker. Nurses leave a little piece of themselves with every patient they care for, be it large or small. That larger, whole internal caring piece is chipped away leaving a trail behind every Nurse to such a degree that soon there is nothing left to give. It has been compared to the bucket being full at the onset of a career, and if no one is refilling that bucket it eventually is totally emptied. Nurses are the last people to refill their own buckets but instead, spend their days filling others' buckets. That is the nature of the person who chooses to dedicate their lives to the care of others. It is also the definition of the job of Nursing, caring for others. Whatever the reason, they are just physically and emotionally done in!!

What is in store for the person who has decided to become selflessly dedicated to learn and train to be the best possible Nurse out there, with no preconceived idea of what is before them? First of all, there is the required monumental funding of the education, secondly, no real understanding of how long it will take to complete all of the training, or what all is involved in the training. There is no idea of what shocking and disappointing surprises, as well as wonderful personal gifts of growth and experiences, lie ahead! One must forge ahead if truly dedicated to see what is out there. It is all about perseverance, endurance, patience, tolerance, personal commitment, and a lot of strength and fortitude…oh, and a really strong stomach for some pretty nasty things. One must have a genuine love of people of all kinds, conditions, and temperaments, and a willingness to give oneself to others. If all that is in place, one of the richest and most rewarding careers can be enjoyed in Nursing.

Now, I come from the day when there were almost no male Nurses. Men were doctors, women were Nurses, period. There were male orderlies, or male Nurse Aides, but not many male Nurses. In that day also, we called upon male orderlies to provide the discreet male tasks such as rectal temperatures, baths, or other procedures necessary for male patients. Nurses did NOT intrude into that male space and cause any kind of embarrassment for our gentlemen patients. It was unheard of. We cared for female patients and our male counterparts were called in to do the sensitive care for the men. We have come quite a long way since those days as today we have, pretty much, as many male Nurses as female Nurses and orderlies have gone their own way and are now well-trained and Certified Nurse Assistant's. Everyone takes care of assigned patients and it is totally non-gender related in most medical arenas.

One of the practical gifts of Nursing is that anyone can find a Nursing job anytime, anywhere. It is a career that has experienced very few layoffs, downsizing, or been impacted in any way by a bad economy. Patients are always going to be there and hospitals will always require staffing levels of Nurses that will assure jobs for any well-referred Nurse who is currently practicing and interested in working.

Military enlistment and training is both available and affordable for anyone desiring to get an education in Nursing. Nurses are very desirable in that field. Entering into the Military today with a degree in Nursing assures one rank, as appropriate to that education, and some pretty good assignments and benefits as an officer and Nurse.

Nurses can move around the world receiving reciprocity for licensure, practice internationally, and experience a wide mobility. I personally have relocated from my home state to another. I simply contacted the State Board of Registry in the new state, paid my required fee, and upon arrival at the new state of residence, drove to the registry office, picked up the copy of my license, and went right to work. In these days of job tensions and unemployment, someone choosing to go into the Nursing field is making an extremely smart choice.

Interestingly enough those aspects of my career choice never crossed my young mind when making my decision. It was one that would impact my whole life and livelihood forever. I have to admit that it was not totally thought out at my young age of seventeen, but someone up there must have been guiding me, as it was a wise choice!

Nursing certainly seems like the way to go for a successful and fulfilling future. To the naïve and vulnerable young girl or guy who is ready to achieve the goal of Nursing, go for it! Make it happen.… but before launching please take note of some of my own personal experiences, both good and bad, that have made me truly proud to have become the Nurse I am today. It has been long, stressful, exciting, ever-challenging, fulfilling, costly, but so very worthy of the trip! I have shed many tears of happiness and sadness along the way. If I had not, then I would not be the Nurse I am today or ever. It has been a really wild and rough ride at times, but a well rewarded effort, in my opinion!

WHAT I DID NOT WANT TO DO!!!

Now, as a sixteen year old high school junior in a small town high school, I had the good fortune of being hired at the only local theater. It was located right down in the center of town on main street, USA. Everyone in town went to this theater for movie nights. An old red-headed spinster was seated in the outside ticket booth selling tickets and admitting everyone wanting to see a movie. She had been there, I understood, from her own girlhood! I was, and am today, a real people-person. I enjoyed seeing all my friends and their dates as they came for a movie and I loved what I was doing.... working in the concession stand. Okay, now this was not something I could see myself doing for many years after, and certainly not as long as the aged spinster out front, for sure! I was certainly way too young to discern between "job" and "career" paths but I did not want a lifetime of serving up popcorn, candy, and sodas! I just wanted to make some spending money and pass my summer with some new experiences under my belt. It was mostly about the money I would have to spend on myself!

Somewhere along the way I knew there was a career....not a job....a career, waiting for me. I was smart, energetic, college-bound, and loved being with all kinds of people. I just knew that I wanted something more than what I had been doing this summer! I wanted to serve as a kind and giving person but had not actually entertained any idea of any specific career choice. I thought about secretarial work, but found it a bit boring and redundant. I considered hair

5

styling just like most girls my age did but I have never had much patience with my own hair, let alone someone else's, so that was scratched out immediately. I felt that I did not have the patience for teaching or working with students of any age, so that was not to be considered. Not being musically or athletically inclined, those choices were not an option either as a career choice. Women were not in the larger workforce in the early 1960's, particularly in the South. Women mostly just married and raised families. I wanted more than that but was not sure what! Ah, Youth!!

I STICK MY TOE INTO THE OCEAN OF NURSING!!

CHAPTER 3

Actually, I cannot recall when I first felt the urge to become a Nurse. I think it must have been during my high school years, as that is when I made the decision to take a high school class offered called ICT (Industrial Co-operative Training). Now this was typically designed as a class for those students who have limited aspirations, as well as funds, for college, therefore, training for a more occupational type career while in high school was more sensible for them. It also was a convenient class worth several credits for those of us who had satisfied all our graduation requirements for our senior year but were mandated to continue attending classes while still in school waiting for graduation. I was not eighteen yet therefore I could not register for college so I was best served to just continue going to High School for full days until the end of May.

With all my other graduation requirements satisfied, I registered for the usual senior classes of English IV, Chemistry II, Algebra II, and still had a half day to do with as I pleased. The school Counselor suggested that I consider one of the courses offered as one of the "on-the-job" training classes in ICT. It would help prepare me for college in the Fall, while meeting the requirements of the full-day attendance mandatory for graduation.. I looked over the list of choices in ICT provided by the school registrar....dental assisting, automobile upholstery, auto mechanics, hospital laboratory assisting, dry cleaning, floral arranging, and many various and uninteresting

7

areas, and to my mind, equally boring vocational opportunities. Finally, there it was….. Nursing Assistant! Maybe in that job I just might be able to see what it was that Nurses do, give some actual educated thought to becoming a Nurse, keep up with all the local gossip in the hospital, and still meet all the required graduation requirements! In effect, it would afford me the opportunity to see if Nursing could be a career for me!

With this information in hand, I signed up for ICT, and was the designated Nurse Aide in the class. How bad could it be, I thought, right? It beat boxing popcorn and pouring sodas in a movie theater, for sure!

Okay, you have to understand the dynamics of the little town I lived in and what everyone was like. It was a typical small southern town with only one hospital (the one I happened to also have been be born in) staffed only with local Doctors, Nurses, and clerks from our busy little town. As there were no Nursing Education programs in town, anyone wanting to pursue a Nursing degree had to move to a larger town to accomplish this. At that time this felt very daunting to me! I was a very small town girl!

You also have to understand that in this day and time, any young woman (and remember it was primarily women entering into Nursing at this time) who wanted to become a Nurse could NOT get married. What!?! It was not allowed, and Nursing students lived in a dormitory-type Nursing Residence. I was, of course, in love with my high school sweetheart and the thought of surviving without marrying him for three or four more years was devastating and totally unthinkable to me! Well, I would just continue being just a Nurse Aide for now, date my sweetheart, and work it out after graduation from high school.

Now, let's get back to our small town. Everyone knew everyone else and on any given day you could go to the hospital, walk up and down the halls, go from room to room, and visit just about everyone you knew who were hospitalized. This included families from school, church, our local grocery store, and work. Local Ministers did this everyday, visiting people from their congregations and serving the whole community with support from their various houses of worship. It was virtually the unacknowledged social hub of the town, except perhaps our churches, or downtown on the square where old men played dominos under the big oak trees all day.

My sweet Mother really was proud, feeling that I had actually arrived at a decision critical to my future. Someday as a Nurse, I could walk those sanctified halls in charge of the hospital. My Father, however, let me know right away in no uncertain terms that he felt that I "did not have what it took to become a REAL Nurse, what with all the blood and frightful sights that Nurses have to contend with." I just thought he was foolish, that it really was not that big a deal, and it should be an awful lot of fun! I did not give him the credit he deserved, I have learned since. Again, just how bad could it be, right? Boy! I had a lot to learn!

So, for all the reasons you can and cannot imagine I began my long journey toward a Nursing career at the tender age of 17 years, in a small town under the watchful and sometimes scrutinizing eyes of a lot of people that I did not want to disappoint! After all, what do parents know about us and what we aspire to become as young adults? They could NOT possibly know enough about us to determine where our successes and failures might emerge, right?

We all know that every job of importance has a uniform, such as businessmen, firemen, policemen, military, or even a pretty dress worn by secretaries. Nursing is no different, but the uniform of a Nurse is special. The white uniform of a Nurse seems to actually glow! Pure white for a profession that is so very pure. It represents cleanliness, caring, and dignity. Nursing Assistants also have a uniform that is standard to the facility served. Keep in mind that this was the very early 1960's and "scrubs" were reserved only for the staff of operating rooms and recovery rooms. Scrubs, also, were certainly NOT worn all over town, and not covered in animal prints, hearts, flowers, and all the fabrics you see today. They were boring and green with the name of the facility stamped all over them. The uniform that I was required to don, and so very proudly wore, was a little white pinafore, light blue gingham checkered blouse, and white hose and shoes. Okay, set with a uniform and a pen in my pocket I was all ready to go! I was a real practicing Nurse Aide! I was very proud, immaculately clean, with shiny polished practical white Nursing shoes and pure white stockings.

My ICT Coordinator arranged my interview with the Director of Nursing at the hospital, I went into her office and shared my enthusiasm with her, she dictated my duties and responsibilities, and I was all ready to go. I would be paid $.50/hour for my time there, and magically my name was penciled in on the duty roster! What enthusiasm and pride I took in that! It was a really exciting time for me, and I looked forward to beginning this new stage of my young life. I just knew I could do it, and do it well!

After being released at noon at the High School I hurried off to the hospital to report for duty! I had only thirty-five minutes to have a quick lunch, change into my little uniform, and get out onto the Nursing unit to report to the Charge Nurse. It was stimulating to feel that everyone on that unit was waiting eagerly for my arrival and capable assistance, and how would they ever manage to get it all done before I arrived each day? Just fine, I now suspect, but what an awesome feeling for a young girl of 17, with giant dreams and plans, feeling so very self-important!

It was an exciting time in my life and I had no idea of the path I was headed down. Over the years, I have watched myself grow, learned many lessons, finely tuned my moral compass, and now fully understand the importance of what we do as Nurses for others. It has been a life-altering journey!

I MAKE MY BIG HOSPITAL DEBUT!!

CHAPTER 4

It is important that you understand the Emergency Room is the central hub of activity in a small town hospital even today. Being young, interested, and extremely nosey, this would inevitably be where I would most frequently be found. I found it curiously energizing, exciting, and frightful all at the same time!

One of the first events that I recall in my burgeoning young career was the arrival into the Emergency Room of an elderly man who was seriously injured. You see, I tended to hang out and nose around wherever I thought the action was. I can only hope at this later time in my career that my own little duties and responsibilities were fulfilled as I tarried elsewhere out of curiosity! This old gentleman was found on the local railroad tracks having been struck by a slow-moving train. As the ambulance brought him in I saw that his left arm and leg were badly mangled and very bloody. He was screaming and crying in agony and I had never in my life seen anyone suffer so. I watched in fascination and awe as the very efficient Nurses and Doctors prepared him for surgery and whisked him away to the operating room. I guess the most surprising thought I had at the end of the day was the fact that I had not felt nervous, upset, or queasy. It was shocking to me that I recalled the day's events with caring curiosity and empathy, having only the strongest emotions of desire to help this man in severe pain. I recall having no fear or distaste, but very much wanted to help fix what had befallen him. Maybe I did have what it took to be a Nurse! Just maybe I could do this!

The next day as I made my extremely important rounds on the unit with crushed ice and water, I stopped in at the old gentleman's room and chatted with him. He had no visitors and I learned later that he had no family or friends, as he was homeless. Apparently he was locally known for drinking and sleeping about in the doorways of our town and tolerated as a person who was unemployed and needy, a "beggar" by social standards of that time. I sat down for a few minutes to ask how he felt and if he needed anything that I could offer him. I have to admit I was most curious as to what happened to place him on a railroad track, and what it must have felt like to be hit by a train and survive. I do not recall his reply but he sincerely responded to me by asking me to scratch his left foot, saying that it itched terribly! After looking, I could see that this was the very leg that he had lost to this tragic accident and that leg was now gone. I was pretty shocked that he thought he had a left foot but in my young wisdom I did the only thing I could think of to do and that was to gently rub the dressing where the stump ended just above that gentleman's knee. He was very grateful, thanked me profusely, and off he went to sleep. Maybe I, in some small way, was therapeutic for him! For many years after that I would see the old man hobbling around town on his crutches without a left leg and left arm, and I felt that just perhaps I had contributed to his healing at some level! This healing art just might be my thing!

On another occasion I was again nosing around in the Emergency Room, where I continued to be found, and another patient was admitted by ambulance. She was a young woman perhaps in her thirties who had been escorted by ambulance and State Troopers to our hospital. She had been out alone several nights earlier, and left with an unknown man, was molested, beaten, and dumped in a wooded area on the edge of town. She had lay out in the woods unconscious and bleeding, exposed to the elements for four days, until local "coon-hunters" and their dogs found her. She had been bitten by many insects and small wild animals, and was ravaged, dirty, and in pain. You just have to imagine what an impression this left on me, a young and sheltered small town girl! With careful direction by the

ER Nurse, I washed and dried her scratches and iced her bruises, but was too fearful to even talk with her. She sobbed and agonized, but was grateful to the ministrations I was providing. Amazingly, I found that I actually seemed somehow to feel the depth of her pain. I realized at that time that everyone needs this kind attention when suffering, and I could certainly get used to providing this to them. I remember experiencing some bad dreams for several weeks afterward, and I never learned of her or her assailant's outcomes. It did make me more cautious, and certainly more aware of the dangers lurking out there.

The Emergency Room Chief Nurse was a short, chubby, redheaded lady who had worked in this small town ER for many years and had grandchildren my age. Now I can only imagine what a nuisance I must have been as a curiosity-seeker in her area! She, however, always was so very kind, helping me to develop an early learning process and desire to serve as a Nurse Aide on the track of becoming a real Nurse. She often involved me in the appropriate care of some of her ER patients. I now suspect these were the ones that I had the most to learn from, just like the aforementioned patient. She shielded me like a mother hen, not involving me in the care of the patients that I might unknowingly cause further harm, be confused by, discouraged by, or frightened of. She was a wise woman for me whose immense wisdom has certainly grown in my eyes since. Thank you, kind Nurse, as you likely never knew what an impression you made on my young, naïve mind. You were the Nurse I aspired to be and hope I have achieved.

Some may call me nosey but I prefer to call myself a curious over achiever. I am constantly looking in places I have not necessarily been invited. I want information and to know if I can help in any way. I want to be ahead of the game and know what is going on around me, so I guess maybe I am just a little bit nosey. I still have that curiosity today and it has served me well throughout the years overall. I have learned lessons along the way and developed some improved behavioral filters that have polished my growing professionalism. I have also learned some boundaries, and learned when to mind my own business! Today it is termed staying in your own lane. I am still working on that one, and hope to achieve it before retiring. Aging is one of the best teachers!

OKAY, NOW I AM REALLY LOOSE IN THE HOSPITAL!

CHAPTER 5

Sometimes I actually could be found in the unit that I was assigned to, wandering from one end of the hall to the other, serving fresh ice water or coffee, expertly watering flowers, delivering get well cards, and spreading my excellent healing ministrations of youth. My duties were assigned by the Charge Nurse, but my wanderings were my own and rarely noticed. That, in itself, lets you know just how important I was!

To fully understand what the times were, as you recall, it was the racially charged 1960's. In any hospital, the families "of color" were admitted and treated in a completely different wing of the hospital. Even patients delivering babies were segregated into the "colored" unit. As part of my duties, and in my meanderings, I would wander down to this area of the hospital and into the rooms of the new Moms. I went into the room of a sweet middle-aged "colored" woman who had delivered her seventh baby just that morning. Now to me this seemed like an awful lot of kids to have at home, as I had only one younger sister in our family. She was sitting on the side of the bed feeding her newborn, with a big smile on her face. As I visited with her and admired her new baby I inquired about the sex of her new infant, and she said that it was another girl. I then asked her what she had chosen as her new daughter's name. She grinned broadly and said that this was her fifth girl, and commented that she had about exhausted all the girl names she could think of!

She had considered many names for several months without much success. She quickly followed up with the comment that during her delivery she had heard a Nurse use a word that had a nice ring to it, and that she thought she would use it as her newborn little girl's name...."Placenta". As I was not very knowledgeable in biology at the time, and was not familiar with the word "placenta" personally, I thought it sounded okay to me. I complimented her on her choice and went on my very important way! After all these years and gained knowledge, I shudder to think that some lovely woman born in the early 1960's is going through life with the name Placenta! She must be a very patient woman, and love her Mother so very much!

Another of my visits with new Mothers led me to a lady who had chosen the name Formica Dinette for her little girl.....it sounds pretty and girlish, right? I have certainly heard a lot of creative names through the years! Let's see.....Jim Beam, Jack Daniels, George Jones, Elvis, Jeremiah Johnson, Liz Taylor, Michael Jackson, Chernobel, Emer Gency, and Chlamydia, to name a few.

As I continued my very therapeutic rounds in another unit, I was sent to the room of a young truck driver from the local paper products industry who had been involved in a very severe local trucking accident. He had finally graduated from ICU, after several weeks of intense and specialized medical care. He was in a private room and alone. I had no idea what his condition was, and had been asked by his primary Nurse to take him a cup of coffee. I was to support and help him drink it without burning himself. He had just begun to be able to have food and drinks. As I arrived with his carefully prepared coffee, I was so shocked by what I saw that I dropped the coffee and ran from the room! The nice looking young man was literally suspended by his skull by what I interpreted as "ice-tongs" (like those I had seen at the local ice plant). He was lying in his bed suspended by "Crutchfield Tongs", a treatment for his broken neck. Large weights at the foot of the bed held him suspended with a complex pulley system of cables that were swinging free. I was horrified by what I saw and I could never go back and be of any assistance to this patient again.

I even briefly considered and respected the concerns that my own Father had expressed, and that he just might be right. Being his own daughter, strong-willed and stubborn, I had a mission to fulfill and a point to prove, so I simply avoided this patient from that day forward. I could get past this, and when the time came I would be better prepared for patients like him.

Nursing means a complete lifespan of health care, and the ones that are the most ill and in the worst conditions actually need us most of all. Did I ever have a lot to learn! I did, however, learn through the years that I could choose my specialty within the field of Nursing. I later chose to go into Maternal and Child Healthcare and Women's Health which is where I found my niche. I never was able to develop a comfort zone for Intensive Care, Orthopedics, or even the beloved Emergency Room, where I found my first curiosity sated.

Every one of us have our Nursing comfort zone, and the care of women in childbearing is my place. I could care for the most gravely ill, complex, perinatal patients, and their newborns. I would work hours on end in a unit dedicated to the safest and healthiest outcomes for these patients. I would love it! Nurses must be trained and prepared educationally, provided a broad range of opportunities of experience, and I was no where near that level yet. I had a lot of work to do!!

PERSONAL CONNECTIONS AND A GLIMPSE OF UNDERSTANDING!!

CHAPTER 6

During this time, in late October of 1962, my elderly paternal grandfather, a widower, was diagnosed with advanced lung cancer (he had never smoked a day in his life!!), and was admitted onto the unit in which I so gallantly served. In fact, I had driven him from the small home he had shared with my deceased Grandmother for over fifty years, to the hospital for his admission, after a visit to his personal physician. I had watched him pack a small bag, say goodbye to his little dog Dicey, lock up the house, close the gate telling Dicey to take care of things for him, and walk away from his life as he knew it.

I watched him deteriorate over several weeks but visited him, reading to him daily. I do not remember much about his decline and death in the end and also do not remember being traumatized by this. He bravely faced each day with a smile and took it all in stride. He was a strong and spiritual man. He was prepared to cross the rainbow bridge and be with his wife of many years, who had gone before him. He was ready.

He was a fine old man, and having lived a full and eventful life, and went to his end with dignity and serenity, reading his bible daily. I know I added to his end-of-life final experience just by being his granddaughter at his side reading and caring about him. I have often wondered if I would have given him this time of love and support at his bedside if I had not been "working" on the Nursing unit where he was a patient. Being a young girl of 17 years, I seriously doubt that I would have found the time to spend with him. I have always believed that I was a Nurse to him even then. I had nothing to do with medications he took, IV's that sustained him, or any of the other professional medical supports provided him. What a gift to a loving grandfather who was reaching his own final hours, but to have someone from his family sit and read to him, a lonely old man in his last days.

He spent day after day in an "oxygen tent", a large and unfriendly contraption that separated him from those of us who loved him, but he chugged along in that environment, loving the time I spent with him in his end. He declined any further "fancy" treatment other than those to provide comfort for his breathing, with no last days of intravenous fluids, just sips of water to maintain his fluid intake. He ate little cups of gelatin, drank juice and water, all at room temperature, as was his belief. He had always told me, "Never drink anything hotter or colder than rainwater and you will be okay, girl"....and he lived his advice. He felt that hot or iced liquids were not good for anyone. We honored his beliefs and they served him well to his end. It is all about a peaceful end and the respect of choice in care, based on beliefs carried throughout life. He departed in calm and serenity, with dignity and pride of accomplishing a good life.

In the years to come, I was to lose three other grandparents in this local hospital at different times in my life. I realized, when notified, while living in towns and states far away at a much later age in my life and career, that the loss of these loving family members in this hospital brought a comforting thought. They had great faith in the care and treatment they received in this facility, and I know in my heart that they went to their final rest with love, familiarity of surroundings, and kind attention.

In those days, rather than a hospital chaplain visiting the ill patients in the hospital, their own church leader, or pastor in our case, came daily to that hospital to offer prayers and comfort to the members in their congregation. This not only included new births but also those who were ill, had surgery, and who were living the last of their days in this facility. They prayed together, the minister told a few corny jokes to cheer, and it was an uplifting visit for all. I don't know about everyone else but I sure miss that aspect of hospital spiritual care. I have learned this is a critical piece of the healing process and provides loving support for the end of days. We cannot replace people in the healing process for patients.

MY FIRST PAID NURSING JOB!

CHAPTER 7

Sometime during Christmas Break from school in December, 1962, I was working on my assigned unit. I was approached by the Director of Nursing. She asked to meet with me in her office and said she was so very proud of my enthusiasm and energy for the Nursing field. She said that she would like to have me work for the hospital on a paid basis during the upcoming three month summer break, while I waited to enter college. It seemed that I was being offered $125.00 per month, working eight hours a day, Monday through Friday. Well now! It only took me a moment of brief calculation to determine that it was an offer that I could NOT refuse! So, upon graduation from high school, I became a REAL paid Nurse Aide for our local hospital. I was on my way to my dream!

My first scheduled week I found my name actually written in ink, not pencil, on the unit schedule and posted on the bulletin board!! I was assigned to Central Supply. It was upstairs, next to the operating rooms, recovery room, and the delivery room. This is the unit where all hospital supplies, sterile trays, and instruments were cleaned, wrapped, and sterilized. Other supplies were distributed to each Nursing unit according to received requisitions. I delivered these supplies, helped with the washing, wrapping, and preparation of sterile supplies, while not being allowed to tamper with the dangerous sterilizers, as I could "blow the whole place up!" What I was, it seems now, was a "dishwasher", and eventually would become the official wrapper of sterile instruments and supplies. This provided me with a basis of learning about sterile supplies and where they come from.

I was taught to make coffee for the doctors and surgical crew next door every morning when I arrived at 7AM. One of the first mornings I arrived I washed and cleaned all the parts of the coffeepot and put all the used coffee mugs in to soak. After washing these and some funny looking red things that looked a lot like red rubber donuts, I placed them all on the towel on the counter to dry. While loading my little cart with supplies to begin my rounds to deliver to all the hospital units I heard a loud shriek!! The Nurses from next door had arrived to get their morning coffee and had discovered the little red rubber "bagels" things drying with their coffee cups. To my total and naïve surprise, I had washed their coffee cups with rubber "pessaries". Since, I have learned that these were removed from female patients, having previously been inserted to support the uterus in the pelvic floor. These Nurses were much less than pleased, and when they explained what the little red rubber things were, I was mortified right along with them! They were, however, most forgiving. How could I have known? Someone else took over the coffee making detail for awhile, and everyone was very careful to keep the operative supplies away from the coffee counter from that day forth!

During my designated and very important rounds to check which patients were using their wall oxygen daily, I answered the call light of a young woman on the second floor. I quickly recognized her as having been frequently admitted and discharged off and on since I had worked at the hospital. I had seen this lady being brought into the hospital in various states of mental disarray, often by ambulance, restrained and hysterical, and always without any family. It was my young interpretation that she was apparently not mentally stable. She was under the care of the local psychiatrist and had frequently been confused or anxious when I saw her in the admission process.

When she turned on her light, I felt that I was competent to answer her requests and help her with her patient needs. As I entered her room she was sitting on the bed crying. I asked her if I could help her and she asked me to look out her hospital window and tell her what I saw. I looked out and seeing nothing other than the local landscape, told her so. She then asked, "Do you see me suspended in space lying in a coffin?" I looked again and said, "No, I don't see anything like that." Now you can only imagine the relief I saw in that woman's face when I assured her that I saw nothing. She then added, "You know I am crazy, they all say that I am, so I guess I must be." In my most therapeutic voice and feeling very much the professional healthcare provider, I curiously asked her, "What is it like to be crazy?" In her calm and unruffled voice, without even batting and eye, she quickly and easily looked me in the eye and answered "Have you ever had a really scary bad dream?" I replied, "Of course, I think everyone has." She then said, "Well, just imagine having that bad dream and never ever being able to wake up from it!" Wow! That was frightening to me and I pondered it only as a young girl could, but I do recall feeling deep empathy and caring for this beautiful troubled soul. I am not sure whether I set her treatment plan back by decades, or if just maybe I helped her by asking such a naïve and innocent pointed question! I then sat down in a chair in the room and was just quietly with her for awhile. Soon she lay down, fully clothed, as she always was, and fell asleep. Only then did I feel that it was okay to leave her. I frequently checked in and said hello to her when near her room just like an old friend would. I only hope that she somehow found some peace in her world at some future point in time.

I first observed the birth of a child there at the hospital where I, myself, had come into the world only 17 years earlier. Actually I was not really invited, as usual, but only peeked unobserved through the small glass window of the delivery room door. I was appalled by the loud noises that the lady was making in the small labor room before going into the delivery room. I did not go to her, as I was frightened and unsure of what I would say or do. As I peered into the window of the small, brightly lit, sterile-looking room, and as they held up the wet, messy screaming infant and began to dry it off, I realized, for the first time, just how totally comfortable I was with this, and somehow could really get into this aspect of Nursing! I cannot ever remember being frightened or even uncomfortable when attending the birth of a baby. From this first one in the summer of 1963, until the last one I assisted into the world sometime during the early 2000's it felt right. Somehow I felt that I had done this many times before. This was so very familiar to me and I was totally comfortable with it. The love and encouragement a young mother to be needs during labor and delivery seemed to be second nature to me, and I only regretted not being able to be a bigger part of it that day!

After that, every time I discovered a lady in the nearby labor suite I managed to slip in to her room during her labor and hold her hand, reminding her of how well she must be doing. Maybe it was then and there that I truly felt my calling as an Obstetrical Nurse! This feeling was to lead me into the most profound, fulfilling aspect of my career. I began that journey in 1967 and worked as an Obstetrical Nurse throughout my career in teaching hospitals that delivered as many as 650 babies per month, and small community hospitals that only delivered as few as 50 babies per month.

I love the whole circle of life, particularly the perinatal aspect of women's lives. It is a happy place to be most days, but can also be the most profound sadness one can experience when things do not go well. I honed and developed my skills in the mother-baby areas, becoming a Nurse who could spend a career celebrating life from the beginning. I had found my niche, for sure!

EVERYONE NEEDS ROLE MODELS!

CHAPTER 8

Okay, now back to the young Nurse wannabe working toward a career in Nursing.

Another person that I personally deemed a hero on a pedestal was a grand old Registered Nurse who had worked at this little hospital since she had returned as a Nurse from World War II. She also was the old Nurse who had, 25+ years later, stood stoically at all four of my beloved grandparent's bedsides at their deaths in the same hospital. She was a Nurse who seemed to me to be at the hospital every day, all shifts, in charge of everything and everyone in the building at all times. She was an "Old Maid", having never married to anything but her Nursing career. I found her amusing, tough, majestic, knowledgeable, all-seeing, and very starched and stiff! You could have cut paper with any Nursing uniform garment she proudly wore, from her tall Nursing cap, with the severe black stripe, down to her uniform, which fell well below her knees and just above her clunky heeled white clinic shoes. These clinic shoes were spotlessly shined with polish, and NEVER soiled or scuffed! Her thick support hose could have supported even the most bulbous and profound varicosities!

I loved her dearly and she had loved, healed, and supported my own family, both parents' sides, through the toughest of times. She was always there for us through good and bad times. In the early 1950's she had her tight hair curls done by my favorite Aunt for the past two decades at the local beauty shop. I always felt that she held

26

a special fondness for me....either through birthright, family history, my obvious admiration of her, or my apparent strong desire to follow in her Nursing footsteps.

Another Nursing hero of mine was the Director of Nursing for this facility, who was one of the youngest career Nurses that I had ever known. She was likely in her early 30's, but compared to most of the local nurses, anyone under 40 was, in my eyes, very young. This lady was the one who had enough confidence in me to invite me to work for the hospital during my summer break after graduation in 1963.

She made a lot of suggestions for schools of Nursing for me to consider in my Nursing education plans. She was a wonderful role model, and often spent time with me in her office talking about my fine choice of a Nursing career, and offering good insight and guidance.

One of the best pieces of advice she gave me occurred when she had to call me into her office and discipline me for some infraction, now forgotten. When I was nearing tears upon being corrected, she kindly told me that "to appreciate a corrective criticism from a superior is to be taken as a compliment in the highest degree, and is one of the finest attributes you can develop". She explained that she cared enough for me to make me a stronger and wiser person, and in my future as a Nurse there would be many, many times I would stand corrected or be called upon the carpet. It would be to my advantage to be able to take that corrective action from this Nurse, and grow from it, knowing that it is delivered as an act of love and growth, therefore making me a better person and Nurse. I have carried that advice with me for more than fifty years, having often experienced just what she explained. I deem it some of the best advice ever received. Take corrective criticism and thank that evaluator, knowing that it is an opportunity. I have also shared this bit of advice in my career, in both supervision and team Nursing. Worthy advice! She was a wise woman. She also was kind and patient with my youthful questions and clinical curiosity. What a different style she practiced from the old family Nurse that I also admired! I grew comfortable that the career I had chosen would allow me to be new, innovative, kind, rigid in my practices, as well as professional. These two fine ladies gave me confidence, along with a sustained belief system in the personalization allowed and engendered in Nursing as a career. They were excellent role models for a young girl, who was now almost 18, pursuing a new direction in life.

Nursing is a noble career and anyone going into it must love it or leave it. I love it, and have always felt proud to be a Nurse who is dedicated and knowledgeable. I only hope that somehow I have influenced someone else to take my place in Nursing when I can no longer perform and care for my patients well. I would aspire to the idea that someone somewhere will be saying that they remember something I told them that truly made a difference in their life. To leave a positive footprint in this world is what we all should aspire to.

OFF TO COLLEGE!!

Sometime during the last days of my final school year in that warm, beautiful May springtime of 1963, I walked across the stage of my local high school and graduated in my little hometown. There was absolutely no question in my mind as to what my career would become.....Nurse. I had somehow managed to convince my Father that I could and would become a Nurse, so we went about the business of choosing a college for me. Now we were not rich by any means, but he was dedicated to sending me to a fine school where I felt I could master this education and career. We looked into several four-year colleges, but if you can only imagine what it was like in the early 1960's for Nursing students you will be shocked!

First of all, you must live in the dormitory at the University you have chosen. Secondly, you cannot be married! That comes as quite a surprise to students today, but that was the rule. Remember, I was in love? I had a boyfriend who was attending the University in the small town only twenty five miles north of our own small hometown. We had been dating for about a year, he was a freshman at the University, and commuted daily, while living at home in our small town, because he could not afford to live on campus. I was so desperately in love and could not even imagine my life in another town, much further away, living in a dormitory, and without him! Not when we could carpool, make that trip everyday to the neighboring town to school together, and complete our education together. It was a plan and I was set!

Against my Father's very wise wishes, I chose to go to a one-year Nursing program in the town where the University was located. I would commute with my boyfriend, and become a Licensed Vocational Nurse. Also, a student in this program could be married.... in fact, most of the students enrolled were actually married with families......problem solved, right?

Well, since making this decision I have learned just how smart my Father was, and what a youthfully poor choice I made that year. Now, don't get me wrong, I did become a Nurse, but in my youthful wisdom I settled for less education when it was offered, sorely disappointed my own Father, and neglected to realize that I could aspire to more. He was willing to make a huge financial sacrifice to provide the education I wanted.

I also had the option of going into the military and being trained as a Nurse, but no, I was in love! Silly me!! My dream, apparently, was to get married while we were in school and continue our lives after graduation. In my youth I did not have the expertise to call upon to realize how frightening that was for him, and how unrealistic it was for me. Apparently he was not ready for that, and I was certainly willing but also not ready, so things began to unravel in our youthful relationship, and soon we were not anywhere near on the same page. As you might rightfully assume, within months, we realized that our "love" was not really what it seemed, forever enduring, and our relationship was done. Here I was now with no way to commute, and I still desperately wanted to finish my education. No ride, and out of ideas! Dreams and plans were in the ditch!

Here I sat, out of options, but still with that burning desire to finish my Nurse training and achieve the dream I had aspired to. My Dad, as usual, came through. He bought me an old 1952 Chevy. Now this car was not much, but I drove it between home and school until one day it began making an odd sound in the motor. When I drove it into the driveway at the end of the day, it stopped running and never started again. What a disaster! Dad did what he could to get me where I needed to go and now that option was gone. I suspect he was done, and lay the decisions at my feet, and rightfully so.

I had to figure out how I could complete my training in the other town, and for me quitting was NEVER a viable option! I would have to live there, but where, I knew not. As a young girl of finally 18, I would just have to figure something out. I was confident, and could conquer anything! Time to be a big girl and get on with it!

MY NURSE TRAINING AT THE HOSPITAL!!

CHAPTER 10

Now, while in high school and taking the classes in ICT, I had a schoolmate who was also working at our little hospital as a Nurse Aide. She had graduated from High School a year ahead of me and was going to the same Nursing program I was attending. She had chosen this route due to her lack of funds. She had no family support for herself and was independent and on her own in life. She was living in the University town near the hospital in a tiny little one room apartment, above a garage in a local private home. As she was borrowing money from her older brother to survive day-to-day, she needed someone to share expenses with her and be a roommate. We decided to try this option out. Now, the fact that I had only a monthly income of about $30.00 in stipend from the Nursing school, and a little endowment from my grandfather, and I do mean LITTLE, I thought I could swing it!

I moved up there and we settled in. We walked to and from the hospital the three short blocks everyday, and ate a lot of left over food from the patient trays for our evening meals. We harvested unopened packages of crackers and juice, cartons of unopened milk, and anything we could gather from patient trays for our meager dinners at home in the evenings, as we studied. We never thought of weather concerns, daily needs for nutritious foods, or any potential that we just might actually get sick ourselves.

The classes were long, the study sessions seemed to never end, the

32

partying was often, as we worked and played hard, learning much and growing in both mind and spirit! We were launching ourselves into this wonderful world of healing and we hoped, a career in which we could make our families proud. We were not afraid of financial or career disaster.....we were invincible. All we needed was a jacket for the winter, our clean and ironed uniforms daily, and a little left over food we scavenged for dinner. Life was good and we were young best friends!

It never occurred to either of us that we were about to undertake a career that would take us all through life and have an everlasting effect on not only ourselves, but many friends, relatives, and patients for a great many years to come. Most of these events we experienced I still recall, as we traveled on our road to becoming good Nurses. We were curious, innovative, extremely poor, dedicated, and creative cohorts. We went to a variety of the local University Fraternity parties, with a frat house right across the street from our humble little abode. We learned how to make the best fried bologna sandwich that tasted like gourmet food! We walked or rode with college students who had cars, all over town without fear, and to climb into anyone's car at that time meant a ride, not danger. Life was safe and exciting in that day and time. It was innocent and fun packed with memories. Laundry was hand washed, line dried, and ironed. I look back upon some of the crazy things we did and wonder how we ever managed to make it through.

Our patients, however, always received the most dedicated and respectful care, but our mentors, instructors, and parents must have been so very exhaustingly weary of our young ways! I can only imagine how many worries our parents must have suffered!

The duty roster for the student Nurses was posted in a loose leaf notebook in the foyer of the main lobby of the hospital, and students' clinical assignments were delegated along with all the nurses' daily assignments throughout the hospital. One morning, when my room mate and I arrived for duty we reviewed the assignment roster for our day that had been completed by our Nursing Instructor. Now, this duty roster was written totally in pencil so that assignments could be easily changed based on patient admissions. In most worlds this would be a good idea, but when dealing with young Nursing students, this proved to be not so good an idea. We wanted to be on the same unit for the day. We thought it would be a great idea to just change the assignments, so we simply erased and re-assigned ourselves! I can only imagine now what confusion and frustration that must have caused our Instructor. I don't know if they realized it and chose to ignore it or of they actually just never figured it out, but for us, it worked at the time!

We had duties during those times that now have been replaced by modern technology.....washing, drying, turning, powdering, and cloth wrapping gloves for sterilization. They were placed into the sterilizer, or autoclave, and prepared for use on the next patient. We also washed and ether-dipped glass syringes, carefully sharpened needles, and then wrapped and sterilized the syringe/needle sets for reuse. We washed and wrapped, for sterilization, rubber catheters for reuse. We did not have the privilege of enjoying disposable gloves, syringes, and disposable everything else used on patients that we have today. Nothing was disposable at that time. Everything was reused and only disposed of when badly worn or broken. We student Nurses were the lowest level. Nurses, even beneath Nurse Aides. We did the most menial tasks imaginable, tasks that housekeeping personnel had done in our little hometown hospital. Bedpan flushing, cleaning sinks full of used, bedside equipment, and daily cleanups at the bedsides of emesis basins were most frequently our responsibilities. We were doing the dirty jobs, called learning and experience, and if it was boring, tiresome, demeaning, dirty but necessary, we were assigned to it.

The Nursing Instructor, widow of one of the most prestigious and recognized physicians in this town, was rigid but patient. She was highly respected. She ran a "tight ship", reminding us daily, and sometimes hourly. Everyday, she approached us and reached down and popped the support stockings we were required to wear. Forbid that they should not have a resounding pop! She also weeded out anyone with red or colored underwear beneath our student

Nurse uniform. Many mornings we were sent walking home to change our undergarments to "something appropriate", meaning of course, white. Shoes that were not pure white, un-scuffed, and highly-polished were grounds for severe consequences. Jewelry was a definite criminal offense in her world, and hair was to be clean, up-do if long, and nails short, well manicured, and without polish. We were on her radar all day while on duty, and her professional guidance and role modeling was above reproach! There were NO exceptions to her dress code!

In all due respect to this wise woman, who has surely gone on to her earned reward, I gained my professional respect for appropriate dress in Nursing. I hope she somehow knew that I now thank her often for the fact that even after fifty years of Nursing, I have NO ugly varicose veins in my legs. I still harbor slight guilt when I manicure my nails and put on a coat of bright polish. On the days that I have dressed in brightly colored print "scrubs", slipped into my tennis shoes, and headed off to work in the hospital wearing a fanny pack, I still feel a bit naughty! My Nursing cap is in a place of honor in my home office in a nice plastic carrier, still starched, with a bit of yellowing and curling around the edges. That larger than life Nurse still sits on my shoulder wagging her finger at me when I breach some stoic dress code for Nurses. She lives in my mind with respect and dignity. Times have changed, but my respect for her, and myself, has not.

These days, when we visit the Nursing units within our local hospitals, we see Nurses dressed in a variety of prints and colors, wearing fanny packs, large clog-like shoes or tennis shoes, hair down over their shoulders, and I just have to wonder what our predecessors would deem acceptable. Times are very different now, but certainly we Nurses agree these are so much more practical in dress and style. Florence Nightingale, as well as my old long gone Nurse mentors must be twirling in their graves!!

Everyone recalls the sad times of the 1960's and racial discrimination. I recall that all our "colored" patients were housed in the basement of the hospital, and not delineated by disease process, but instead, color/race alone. Everyone colored was admitted there, including surgical patients, ladies who had delivered babies, the gravely ill elderly, and young pediatric patients. The hospital did have a mother-baby unit upstairs on the third floor, but the babies of color were in the room with their mothers in the basement, after an appropriate observation period. The "white" babies were kept in the nursery upstairs. This came as no surprise to either my roommate or me, for in our small town hospital, this was also the norm for the times. Downstairs in the Cafeteria the "colored" also were served from a different serving line than the rest of the population. Nursing students also ate from this separate serving line.

One day a tall, well-dressed "colored" lady from a really big town in the northeastern part of the United States was visiting family in the hospital. She insisted that she be served from the "white" serving line. Everyone was aghast, and I can only recall standing off to the side while all the administrators hustled around trying to soothe ill feelings. She was accustomed to being served in an integrated fashion and our small town ways were totally unacceptable to her. I do not recall what resolution was afforded, but we Nursing students went on our way feeling somewhat impotent as to what could be done to resolve the issue. As Nurses we failed, even then, to understand the lack of respect shown. To Nurses, skin color is not recognized and patient need is uppermost in our minds. We care for people and their disease process. Remember, this was the shameful 60's and times were, unfortunately, what they were. I see an improved world we live in today in this aspect of humanity, but we still have a way to go.

One real life-altering experience for me on duty as a student Nurse occurred when I was on the Mother-Baby unit and was giving medications. I had my little tray all set up with little medication cups lined up with little medication cards under each one. I had a card to administer an injection of Penicillin to a patient who had experienced a Caesarean section earlier in the week. She was to get this injection every morning for 5 days. The Nurse from the previous day, day 5, had not destroyed the card and I failed to count the days she had received these injections. My error was to not check the orders and verify just how many injections she had already had. I made a medication error and had to own it. I administered the injection and upon return to the Nurse station, realized that I had, in fact, given her a 6th injection. When I reported this to my Instructor and the charge Nurse they immediately told me what I had to do. I had to phone the physician and discuss this medication error, then fill out the appropriate forms. Well, it just so happened that this particular physician was about the oldest, grumpiest, strictest physician on staff. Everyone's knees knocked even when he arrived on the unit! I called him, took a loud and frightening "dressing down" from him, and took my punishment like a big girl! I also vowed to really, really work hard to never make a medication error again as long as I practiced! It was a lofty goal, but hopefully attainable. I will do my best! I have never forgotten that incident, and to this day will tell any Nurse that if you say you have never made a medication error, you either have not given much medication or you are fibbing. We who give medications as Nurses have all made mistakes, and it is one of the most powerful learning experiences you will ever have. It is humbling! Nurses learn to own what they do, go forth carefully, and accurately learn from our mistakes. Nursing must be, and is, based on HONESTY, above all else. Ego, pride, or any other selfish feelings have no place in Nursing. Honesty is critical in all we do. Florence would have been proud of my choices as a young woman that day!

As Nursing students we were assigned to a variety of units, such as mother-baby, nursery, surgery, medical, surgical, and emergency units. We moved throughout the hospital learning about illnesses, administering medications as ordered, having our stockings popped daily, and scrubbing everything around us. We sat with elderly patients who were peacefully passing at the end of a long and hard life, made soiled beds fresh, bathed and comforted patients of all age, sex, color, or religion, rocked and cuddled infants, and held the hands of ladies who were in long, tiring labors. We learned academics, compassion, understanding, and respect for those around us.

Every afternoon we gathered in the Nursing classroom, in a large residence/education building across the street from the hospital, for our classes. There we learned the didactics of medicine, memorized bones, muscles, organs, veins, arteries, and systems in our quest for learning about the human body. We had some pretty grueling and challenging tests in that same classroom, but it was our altar of learning. To learn is to grow and to grow is to learn.

One of my most memorable hours in that Nursing classroom occurred on November 22, 1963. Suddenly and quietly the door opened and the Director of Nursing for the hospital entered our classroom, leaned forward, and whispered something very somber into the ear of our Nursing Instructor. She paled, nodded, and calmly stood and announced to our class, "Ladies, our class is being dismissed immediately. You are excused to go home. Our President, John F. Kennedy, has been assassinated in Dallas, Texas. Please gather your things quickly, move quietly out of the building, and go home to pray for our country. Please wait for further notification as to when we will resume classes." We had no idea what would happen next.

Having no telephone or TV in our little apartment, we somberly went home, prayed for the Kennedy family, our country, and waited until the following day, when we returned to our duty roster at the hospital for further instructions. Later in the afternoon we did go to the fraternity house to watch their television as the unbelievable and disquieting events unfolded after the assassination of our President. We could only wait and pray, as everyone around us felt that a world-altering event was sure to follow. The following morning, as our usual schedule dictated and without any further directives or guidance, we rose, dressed, and went back to the hospital on duty. Within a paralyzed nation we considered it, and felt that should something disastrous happen in our world, the hospital would likely be the best place for us to be. We went to the hospital and waited. Hospital routine went forward pretty much as usual, and we continued our rounds of patient care and duties. That is what Nurses do.

I recall things continued in the hospital pretty much on schedule, but particularly remember the dark cloud that settled over our country for the next several months as we grieved as a nation. We survived this tragedy, but things were not ever quite the same for some time afterwards. It was troubling times!

We student Nurses were aware of the Viet Nam War only by occasional TV and radio, but no one that we were acquainted with served, and our little town was pretty safe and unaffected by what was going on a world away. I look back on it now, currently being married to a Viet Nam Veteran, and wonder how we were so oblivious to the horror of a war that was taking such a huge toll on our American young men. Some say we are lucky to have been spared that heartache. I personally feel a bit guilty for that oblivion we were enjoying, while they were protecting our freedom at such a high price. I am only glad today that I can give thanks often to someone who put his life on the line while I went about my safe life learning to be the best Nurse I could be.

I have learned so much more about politics and what was going on during those times outside our naïve little world. As I have aged and moved through a volatile and razor-edge world, I now have so much respect and appreciation for those who work hard to keep our country free. That will be evident as my Nursing career unfolds though out this narration, and we must hold in our hearts and minds all that has transpired over history. We must forever be grateful, as so many have been lost perpetuating our freedoms for us.

My one regret, as a Nurse. is that of my not entering the military, training, building my career, and fulfilling my Nursing dreams caring for those who fought for our country. It would certainly have taken me down a more dangerous and foreign path, but I can only imagine the good I could have done, being less selfish and giving more of me to my country. Apparently that was not to be, and I can only be the best Nurse I can today. I can remain proud of what I have done.

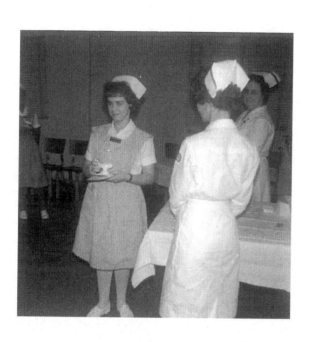

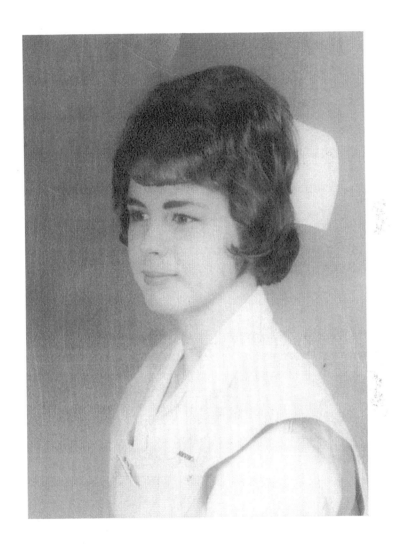

LICENSED VOCATIONAL NURSE....AND THEN FAMILY!!

After a year of hard work and studying, testing, observing and practicing procedures, my roommate and I were finally "capped", "pinned", and graduated out into the big scary world of Nursing. We got our little white Florence Nightingale china lamp with a candle in it, and walked across the stage of the hospital conference room with ten other ladies. We were ready to take our State Board Examinations to become Licensed Vocational Nurses. We had fulfilled a dream. Little did I know what lay ahead!

We took our State exams, passed them with flying colors, and were ready to be Nurses for real. It was a proud moment when I received in the mail my letter and State License to Practice. This exam included both academic as well as clinical practical testing. We were tested on paper, required to achieve an 80% or better. We then were to perform specific procedures before our Clinical Instructor and other seasoned Nurses in a clinical setting, also at an 80% level or greater. Only then were we considered fit to actually care for patients in the hospital. Dreams do come true, with lots of hard work and study! I had NO idea just how far my young desires to become a good Nurse would take me down the road of patient care. This was just the beginning, and I still had a LONG way to go!

Somewhere along the way within the year after graduation and licensure, my room mate and I each married, set up housekeeping, and began our families. Our big glowing dream of becoming Nurses dimmed and fell behind the even bigger dream of marriage and family. After all, we were now educated, 19, and had achieved Nursing as our career. We were willing to put it on a back burner and concentrate on husbands, cooking meals, diapering babies, and child-rearing, but knew we could certainly go back to our shelved dreams anytime we chose. That is what we did back in the 1960's. Marriage and family were very high on the priority list and careers followed a close second. It was a different time then. Men worked, women stayed home and raised the children. Okay, let's see how this goes.

Viet Nam and the draft were in full force, it was profoundly uncertain times for our men, and if we did not grab at life, who knows what might happen. Life was moving very fast, and that is just the way it was in the 1960'. We wanted it all!

I married my young first husband in 1964, gave birth to a beautiful baby girl in 1965, and began my new career as a housewife and mother. I loved being at home with my little girl, and we had wonderful times, but my husband often traveled in his work and I began to miss being a Nurse. I just had to work out how I could have the best of both worlds. I certainly would not feel good about leaving my baby with someone else while I worked, and had no family nearby to support my childcare needs. This went well for about six months.

Suddenly, due to my husband's job, we found our little family moving to one of the largest cities in our state, about one hundred fifty miles away from our small town. Upon arrival in this huge metropolis I felt intimidated by the size. Slowly, I began to drive around and get my confidence up. Being a Nurse seemed to be so far away now. Little did I realize that I was wrestling with the age old concern of choosing between career, or homemaker and mother. Many of us have done this, and it is tough. I missed practicing the skills I had learned and developed, and loved my time with my child too.

After about a year of being a housewife and mother, and as she had grown older, I decided I would find a wonderful day care center for my daughter and go back to my Nursing career. I also felt that my daughter was ready to go out and experience the outside world too, and learn more about life and others her age. She would have fun! I found a nice little local day care center, went out and found a local hospital job as LVN. On the first day to drop off my little one I dressed us, drove over, and handed her off to her new caregivers. As I left the parking lot I looked back and saw her at the window with her little hands up on the window, crying her heart out. What a sad sight! I immediately drove straight to the hospital, resigned, and drove right back to the day care center, picked her up and drove home. We both cried all the way home and I determined that I could do no better job than be her Mother until she was ready to separate from me. She was only 14 months old and I would let her decide when she could do without her Mother. Sometimes it is about priorities, love, and a whole lot of guilt!

That old Nursing siren song was daily in the back of my head. When my daughter was two and a half years old we lived in a nice little apartment complex, with good neighbors who had children her own age, down the way. One Mother and I became good friends and I cared for her child two days a week for her while she worked part time as a Dental Assistant nearby. After a while, my friend was willing to care for my daughter if I wanted to go and work a few afternoons, so with this in place I again decided to re-launch my Nursing career. I felt that I was finally set! I would just work part time and have the best of both worlds being both Mother and Nurse!

SMALL HOSPITAL IN A LARGE TOWN!!

CHAPTER 12

I found that there was a brand new little hospital going to open soon in our neighborhood, just blocks from our home. They were interviewing soon, so here was my chance! I interviewed and was hired into the Mother-Baby Unit of the new facility. Actually I would be working in the Labor & Delivery suite of the hospital! I had absolutely no real experience in this area other than that of a student, and of course new mother, but they were willing and I was excited, so I jumped at the chance!

This was my dream come true! I agreed to work the 3-11 shift, and with my husband out of town often, it worked out well. I could leave my young daughter with my neighbor when both girls were down for their afternoon nap, and she would enjoy her little friend for the evening. I would pick her up after my shift ended and take her home to bed. It could not be a better plan!

I soon began working at the new hospital with all new Nurses, and in the Unit of my dreams. What a great opportunity for me! It was a small 125 bed hospital with a small group of physicians next door, and considered a small community hospital. We all began our job together and quickly developed many close ties within the Unit. We delivered about 15-20 babies per month and I grew so much as a Nurse during my employment in this nice little hospital.

We all know as we plan our lives sometimes we get side-tracked briefly. After beginning work I discovered that I would be having my own second child, to be delivered sometime early in March, 1968. I worked the evening shift delivering other babies daily and continued to dream of my own beautiful baby coming soon. In March, 1968, I delivered a big handsome baby boy! Do I continue to work or do I stay home with my growing family? Well, as I had not resigned but only taken maternity leave, and after enjoying six wonderful weeks at home with my children I was called one evening by the hospital supervisor. She said that they had no one with any experience available to cover the evening shift during the upcoming week. I could not say no. I would be going back! After all, Nursing was my career and in my blood! They needed me and I needed to heed the call! I could work this out!

We had a mature and level-headed teenage girl who lived next door. She came to our house everyday after she arrived home from school and never went home until nearly midnight! She adored our children, and as my husband was still traveling a lot overnight, I came upon a wonderful plan that could meet everyone's needs. She would care for my children in my home after school, paid well, and I could work that evening shift again. It was a great plan that worked well for everyone for over a year, until she left for college. I was able to work on that Labor and Delivery Unit for another year!

I worked with some amazing mentors at this little hospital. One was the Labor & Delivery Supervisor of our small hospital unit, and an experienced Registered Nurse with years of obstetrical experience behind her. She was, by my early 20 year old standard, quite old.... perhaps in her 50's? She kindly led me, patiently taught me, daily supported me, always trusted me, and I grew as a Nurse as a result. I started IV's, examined patients, wrapped supplies, mixed solutions, circulated in the delivery room, and assumed a lot of responsibility. Back in those days we delivered patients without the use of fetal heart monitors, as they were not around at the time. We also administered Pitocin, for inductions of labor, without the use of pumps, but instead, counted the drops of IV solution administered to patients to deliver them. Yikes!

In this day of advanced precautions in place for current Nurses,

I am amazed at the success we had with delivering healthy babies for healthy mothers. Delivering babies was considered something almost anyone could do, and a natural process. Now, I agree that it should be seen as a very natural process, safely monitored, and common sense directed. Today's Standards of Practice are much more tightly monitored, with malpractice at an all time high, caution is the director of all we do. I now believe as Nurses we must have had a cluster of guardian angels hovering over us on a regular basis! I am certain my personal Guardian Angel must have a nervous "tic" by now! I have felt the presence of someone guiding me to a safe end many days and nights, as I have navigated the intricate process of women's health, childbirth, and the care of my patients. We do our educated best, and beyond that it is in the hands of someone greater than we. Nursing is an art to be respected and revered.

One of my profound memories of this unit was of a late evening arrival from the Emergency Room of a lady who was passing through the city. She was in labor and not due to deliver for another six weeks, making her only at 34 weeks gestation. I was alone in the Unit and we had no other patients at the time. We were to rely on the doctor on call, who was easily ten to fifteen minutes away with good traffic. She came in the door of the Labor & Delivery suite in a wheelchair being pushed by a very frightened male orderly. She was crying and very advanced in labor, as I quickly determined by her behaviors and examination. I immediately got her into a bed and as I removed her polyester stretch pants, a tiny, red little pre-term baby dropped into my hands. This child was crying lustily and appeared very active and healthy! I immediately called the Unit Tech to get me some help from the Nursery. We bundled the baby up and got it to the Nursery and into a controlled warmer. I contacted the physician on call, who arrived quickly. We immediately moved her to the delivery room where he could complete her delivery process and get her stabilized and into the recovery area. As I tidied the unit, made the new mother comfortable, and got all the paperwork done, I was stunned and humbled, as this was the very first baby I had personally delivered, completely alone. I went about the job of getting the new mother recovered and moved off to her room on the maternity unit. My shift ended soon, and I went home.

When I arrived the following day on duty I immediately went to this patient's room to check on her and her baby as I often did. They were both doing well, with the baby a premature but healthy child. As I visited with her she took my hand and said to me, "I was so very afraid when I realized that my baby was being born early and in a strange place, and as it was happening so quickly I just watched your face. You were so very calm, I was not afraid. I realized, however, that this was something that you did very often and we were going to be fine." Little did she know that this was my first experience with delivering a baby all by myself and that inside, I was terrorized! I was so nervous but thought that if I panicked she would too, so I just kept it together for her. I have held this woman's words in my heart and mind for all these years since and have had many, many events that were equal to or surpassed that stressful moment in my life. This gives them the courage to get through whatever they are experiencing with the confidence that I can help and support them.

I have even been jokingly accused of "fiddling while Rome is burning" by fellow Nurses when we were experiencing a particularly stressful time on duty. All I can assure them of is that my face is not necessarily showing what my mind is feeling! Believe me, "Rome is burning in my mind!"! Just another learning experience for a young Nurse!

Another experience I shared in this wonderful little hospital unit was one of profound moral testing. It was also a major turning point in my life, when I knew that what I was doing was important and that my decision could affect someone else's life forever. It was up to me to call upon my own strong morals and beliefs, take a gentle stand, and make a difference. I guess it was a major calibration of my own moral compass.

Late one night we delivered a very, very premature handicapped infant who was obviously not going to make it, and I had cared for this mother from her arrival, several days before. At the child's birth, I was instructed by the physician to "just uncover it, turn off the warmer, and let it go". I immediately turned to him and calmly said, "I cannot do that, Sir, as it is not my choice as to when this child passes, and everyone, especially this infant, deserves respect, love, and my attention until the end of its life." I carefully wrapped the baby in a warm blanket, lovingly handed it to the Mother to hold and cuddle, and gave her the experience of holding and loving her baby through its end of life. The next day I went out to see her on the Unit and she thanked me, as she had heard my response and firm stand, and was aware of what was transpiring in that delivery room. She well knew her child was lost, but just to hold and cuddle it to the end meant so much to her. That is why we are Nurses. Not all outcomes are what we would like to see. We can make them somehow easier for our patients just by feeling and sharing the love and empathy that we would want to be shown ourselves. She said she would never forget my kindness, respect, and love shown to her and her lost child.

Profound feelings of loss are normal experiences for Nurses, some days more than others. We give our very best to our patients and do all that we can. I recall one of my mentors wisely telling me during a time of loss, that we cannot save them all. This has supported me and I seek strength from it when feeling that sense of loss. I am a growing Nurse, ever growing through good and bad! "You are NOT going to save them all, and all you can do is do your very personal best" she said. I have thought of that many times, and draw so much from her wise advice, yet today.

SOMETHING DIFFERENT!!

CHAPTER 13

After working on the Labor and Delivery Unit for a year after the delivery of my son I received a wonderful opportunity to work for a local Gynecologist in his office next door. This was something that would provide me an opportunity to have weekends off and work day shift. I now had wonderful day care for both of my children, and they were learning so many new things during their afternoons there. I enrolled them for days and began my new career move into the gynecology field. I was ready for less stress and more growth and exploration into this field of women's health.

I provided this kind and gentle doctor with office help in the manner of chaperone for exams, sterilizing instruments, preparing patients for obstetrical check-ups, and fetching coffee and snacks for the staff. It was a fulfilling year but not too exciting. I did, somewhere in my heart of hearts, actually miss that adrenalin rush of the labor and delivery suite. I guess the most challenging events were getting the doctor out of the office in time to deliver a baby across the street! I did enjoy working with this physician, and when he recruited another partner from Italy I was assigned to him as his Nurse. That was interesting with his speaking Italian and me speaking "Southern". He was single and highly dependent upon someone caring for him. He needed his white coat laid out with pens and prescription pads in the pockets, hot coffee with sugar and cream, to his taste, at his desk when he arrived at the office each morning. I was basically an "office wife" for him, and he was an amazing physician. I, having that need as a Nurse to take care of those around me, enjoyed our office days.

We did some infertility work, some surgical procedures in the office, and it was exciting to see pregnancies evolve from discovery to delivery. I loved seeing the developing fetus even though there were no ultrasounds at that time, throughout gestation. I also enjoyed the return to the office with the beautiful newborns in the carriers. It was a wonderful and bonding experience with these families who were growing with each child born. I occasionally went to their deliveries when invited, and was able to experience the birth with them. I felt very much a part of the whole process.

After a year in this position I was recruited again by another physician. I had taken both of my own children to a local Pediatrician and while at a visit there he asked if I would be interested in coming to work with him and his staff. To sweeten the deal he would provide both my children free medical care!! That, with a better salary offer, was all I needed to hear. I accepted that position, and began my career in the Pediatrics field, with perks!

....AND THE CHILDREN SHALL COME UNTO HIM.....

CHAPTER 14

What an opportunity! He was a much respected local Pediatrician. He provided care for children from birth through 18 years of age. This Pediatrician had been in practice for many years in his community and frequently did pre-college physicals on patients he had cared for since infancy. He had cared for my own little girl from the time we had arrived in this city when she was six months old. He had also provided immediate care for my second child, my son, at his birth and currently. We had a bond of physician-patient that had been sealed for several years and I respected and appreciated his medical expertise beyond all doubt. He was our doctor too, and like part of our family.

We saw many patients every day, a busy office, with emergencies and short notice care for many children. As I had anticipated I had the opportunity to learn how to complete office lab tests, assist in suturing, circumcisions, and taking and processing x-rays. We did allergy skin tests, mixed allergy vaccine, provided immunizations and saw many sick children as well as well-babies. The event of bonding with patient families was wonderful and the children became "my children." Our physician was a dedicated and loving practitioner for children. He was devoted and kind to parents, patients and staff.

One of my most memorable patients was a little girl who was three years old. She had complained of a horrible headache all weekend and when she was brought in to see our MD she was immediately sent to the hospital next door for testing. Upon finalization of Testing, it was determined that she had a malignant brain tumor which was inoperable. We watched her, over a year, decline to her final days, which was one of the saddest experiences of my life. I had a child her age, a beautiful and healthy little girl, and I felt so much empathy for the mother of the child that I cried often with this family in the exam room. This was the first patient for whom I actually attended the funeral, which was a life-altering experience for me, a young mother myself. How does one, I asked my wise and experienced doctor, put your child in the ground and walk away with any measure of sanity? That gentle man said "You do it because you have no other choice, and have to trust in the faith of our Lord that this is happening according to plan, and you will survive it." I never fully understood but my heart broke for this beautiful little girl and her loving family.

Another child we cared for was a little boy, a local physician's son, who had been our patient since birth six years before. He had been born without hip sockets, bladder, and most of his intestines. He had undergone multiple surgeries to have reconstructive procedures done to provide these necessary parts, and at six years old he was very bright, brave, walked with a major limp, but was a jolly child. He had completed most of his surgeries, was walking without a gait walker, and doing well. One Saturday in the summer he slipped and fell into the family swimming pool and drowned before he could be rescued. We all began to wonder why and how he could be taken after all he had been through, after all the medical miracles that the doctors had performed. It did not make any sense at all to me, a young mother. All I could do was hold my own children closer, be the best mother I could be, and pray that I would not have to suffer the kind of losses these parents had experienced.

You have to understand that this office was NOT all doom and gloom. I loved holding these little ones as I weighed them, measured them, diapered them, and gave them the injections that would heal their illnesses or keep them from harm's way. They loved us back and we developed wonderful bonds with the children and parents as they grew. Somehow, in their young minds, they surely realized that what we were doing for and to them was in some way good. They would be healthier and safer for it.

We had several special needs children, with Downs Syndrome, congenial heart disease, and all manner of genetic or congenital disorders. They were all precious to us. One little guy with Downs syndrome who was about two years old when I began work there came in once every month for shots of Gamma Globulin to protect him by boosting his immune system. He was so thin that we Nurses actually went to the back of the office and drew straws to determine who would give his shot each month! We all knew he had to have them, but so dreaded sticking him. We knew it hurt him badly, he did not understand, and we suffered right along with him. He had the saddest little cry, and it was so terribly heart-wrenching to have to hear it. It was heartbreaking, but necessary.

While working in this office I also learned how to do casting for broken arms, breathing treatments for bronchitis or pneumonia, and radiology for foreign bodies (coins, safety pins, etc.) swallowed. It was a wonderful learning experience for me. I also learned how to do day-long allergy skin testing and all manner of injections. We assisted in office procedures every day that saved our patients trips to the emergency rooms of the city, exposing our little patients to many more dangerous diseases.

It was six years of wonderful learning and growing, understanding of pediatrics and childhood issues and needs. I was fortunate enough to be able to administer all my own children's immunizations, as well as allergy testing and other procedures necessary. Little did I know just how it would prepare me for the final chapter in my life in Nursing, one that I would finally be able to retire from when time.

A day in this pediatric office was exciting! When we went to the door to open it and call the next child into the exam room, every child in the waiting room would "freeze" and then run crying to their parents just knowing that it was their turn....and they were terrified! I felt badly about it and tried to ease their fears by being funny and happy, teasing them and coaxing them with the lollipops they always got when they left. The office walls were decorated with life-sized pictures of the various nursery rhyme characters such as Cinderella, Snow White and the 7 Dwarves, Cat & the Fiddle, and the Cow jumping over the moon. It was a cheerful place, full of laughing and crying children. During flu season, or particularly virulent "bug" seasons we would be there for twelve hours, even on Saturdays. These were our children!

Our Physician was of Jewish belief, and every year we had a wonderful Christmas Party, complete with handsome Christmas bonuses and exchanges of gifts, with blended choices of cultural foods from all of our staff. It was fun, and his own elementary age children would attend, and, in fact, be responsible for putting up the lobby Christmas tree! So much for religious wars! It can be accomplished with brotherhood in the world of mixed beliefs, and we had a great mix and even greater time! Besides, we all enjoyed both Jewish as well as Protestant holiday breaks, so it was a good deal for us all around!

The fourth year I worked there our physician had a fairly mild heart attack. He found it necessary to add a new physician to the team to support him while he took some well deserved time off for healing. This new doctor was much slower due to less experience, methodical but equally as good, and we Nurses embraced him. He would tell us funny stories about his completing his medical training in New Orleans by playing a bass fiddle in a band, on one of the famous street's clubs, for money to pay his expensive medical school training. He was a joy!

He was an excellent doctor and many years later my grown up daughter called me from that town we had lived in and asked me what his name was. She said that her insurance company had assigned a pediatrician in town for her two children, aged 2 and 5. She said the name sounded so familiar to her that she wanted to know if this was the same doctor who had cared for her over twenty years earlier. It was! He could NOT believe that he was actually providing care for a second generation of children, and he remembered her well. His last time to care for her was when she was six years old and now here she was bringing her own children to him. What a great reunion!! To my knowledge, he is still practicing pediatric medicine in that town today. Eventually the original Pediatrician retired after many years of practice. What a stellar career! It would be incalculable to determine how many children he served and saved in his long and lustrous career. He was a loving and caring physician and I shall never, ever forget him.

As a family we were given the opportunity to relocate to a new city in the same state with my husband's employment. This would allow both of us a wonderful career growth opportunity, and challenge us with a big change. We chose to go. I would miss my colleagues, kids in the practice, and friends, but it was time to stretch our wings and fly.

We again moved our family to another large city in the state, and now I had a tough decision to make. Was it truly time to move forward with my education in Nursing? Should I find work in this new city and practice my Nursing career? I had some choices to make, and after a summer with my children around the pool and learning our way around this new town I made that call. This decision became obvious.....I needed to get into school and further my education. I would call the universities in town and see what I needed to do to get back into school, further my education, and take that next step.. It was my opportunity to grow now!

COLLEGE-BOUND....AGAIN!!

CHAPTER 15

I so very much wanted to be a Registered Nurse, and not just settle for what I had done so far. I knew I was smarter and capable of more. I wanted to make my family proud and achieve all that I knew I could do. I wanted this very much! I could do it!

I registered at a local college, paid my tuition as I went, and worked very hard to achieve my dream. Dividing my precious time between education and family was hard. My dedication to school and the work involved in completing this degree plan was all-engrossing and it took me away from my husband and family many days and nights. It was a dedication I was committed to in order to be the best Nurse I could be.

I began at the local Community College to attain my ADN, or Associate Degree of Nursing. This would prepare me to sit for the Registered Nurse State Exam. I started in the summer of 1975 with Anatomy & Physiology and Psychology classes. I continued the next Fall semester, completing all the necessary pre-requisites. I then was eligible for application and interview for acceptance into the Nursing Department for completion of the two year Nursing Clinicals. I was nervous, but silently encouraged by the idea that I would be competing with students who had not completed LVN training so I had a sense of impending success. I got my letter of acceptance, and was on my way.....again!

At this time I began taking four semesters of Nursing Courses plus additional electives during the summers in support of them. Each year was more and more challenging as we Nursing students moved about the city doing our clinical practice at a variety of hospitals and in multiple specialties. We took Summer courses in Cultural Medicine and a variety of foreign languages that were commonly spoken in our city.

Pediatrics was done at the local indigent care teaching hospital where children were brought from all over the state, as well as our neighboring country of Mexico. My first patient, for a full week, was a twelve year old boy who had a fractured pelvis from a car accident in Mexico. He spoke little English and I spoke little Spanish so our conversations were exercises in inflection and pantomime! One day as his lunch tray came up and he began to eat, a small boy, about six years old, was sitting next to him in the little patient lounge. The little guy was under-impressed with what he had been served. I asked my young man how to say to the child that he needs to eat his food, and somehow my Spanish changed "Eat your food now, you can play later" became "Eat your dog now, you can float later" and the child ran crying to his room. I was mortified and quickly went to get help explaining what I meant!

At the end of the week, my young man was discharged from the hospital with a lower half body cast. He could only lie down, not sit up, and would be wearing it for two more weeks. His hometown doctor in Mexico would then remove it and he would continue to heal at home. We put him on a gurney and my student partner and I wheeled him down to the exit to meet his parents. It was a cold blustery day in February and as we exited the hospital the family had backed their beat up old truck up to the bay, and had laid blankets in the back bed of the truck. We loaded him in the back of the truck, he had a pillow under his head, and was covered with another blanket. He was all set to head home, about four hours south to Mexico. He smiled broadly and waved happily and was off and gone! We just stood there laughing in amazement! It must have been quite a ride home for him, but he was happy, healing, and headed home!

Another day I was assigned a child about eighteen months old who had pneumonia and had been dropped off in the ER by his undocumented Mother who had returned to Mexico. He was alone and my heart broke for him. When I checked with his primary Nurse she said that his Mom had left the phone number of the little store in her town in Mexico. When he was to be discharged she was to call that number, they would go and locate her at her remote home in the outside of town, and she would make some arrangements to get back to USA to pickup her child. WOW! Unbelievable!

As I prepared to give him his bath and change his linens I noticed a leather strand around his neck with a leather pouch on it. In that pouch was a most odorous "something". I falsely assumed that the whole necklace was causing the awful odor so I took it off and was preparing to dispose of it. The primary Nurse arrived to help me with him and immediately retrieved it and put it back around his neck! Being Hispanic also, she patiently explained to me that it was a preserved deer's eye and if we remove it from him he might die. That is apparently the belief of this particular family within their culture and we must respect their wishes! I made a note to myself to register next semester for another Cultural Medicine class offered at our college. I apparently need to learn much more about our local Hispanic community and their traditions & beliefs! I continued to care for this child until I was rotated off the Pediatric Unit. He was still there wearing his amulet of luck. I guess it worked, as he was getting better!?!

As we progressed through all the Units of the hospitals we were sent to Onocology. My Nursing partner and I were assigned to an elderly gentleman. He was diagnosed with Oat's Cell Carcinoma, a particularly rapid growing form of cancer. He asked us as we arrived to assist him in his morning care, and to please give him a bath, as he had not had one in several days. We prepared the supplies and began with a shave and shampoo and continued the task of bathing him head to toe. About the time we were cleaning and drying his feet we noticed a change in his posture. Upon assessing him more closely, we realized that he had passed away. We were certainly upset, immediately assuming that perhaps we had rushed his demise with our brisk ministrations to his hygiene. Our kind and supportive

Nursing Instructor assured us that we had not, and what a way to go......with a massage and a bath. How relaxing just to have someone touching and talking to you would be an ideal way to cross the rainbow bridge. We were assured that this kind old man met his "maker" clean, freshly shaved, and relaxed!

When we arrived on the Obstetrical Unit of training we were in the "bowels of obstetrics"! We experienced ladies from pre-teens to their fifties giving birth to their first to their seventeenth child, with patients in hallways, corridors, and stairwells giving birth, and one of our Nursing student partners was a young man. At this time he was not married, somewhat of a comedian, very handsome, and certainly not impressed with accommodating the birthing process. He somehow got through this aspect of training with all us ladies' help, and after graduation, joined the Air Force and became one of their top Operating Room Nurses. That is something I could have absolutely seen him do, but birthing, not so much!

During our Obstetrical Clinical process we were assigned patients for whom we had to assess and interview, ask very personal and probing questions, and determine a plan of action for them to follow throughout their pregnancy. Now, mind you, our Instructors were closely overseeing our work and giving us the nod, and suggesting improvements along the way.

I was assigned a patient to develop a Life Health Care Plan with. We as Nurses must consider whole-life needs. We were required to develop a meal plan, medical care plan, and general lifestyle daily plan for them. My patient was a single fifteen year old young lady from Mexico, uneducated, pregnant for the first time, Hispanic, living with her Grandmother who was on food stamps and extremely indigent. Okay, let's see.....we need to deal with: teenager, pregnant, cultural beliefs, poor, uneducated, unmotivated, and with a future child to raise. Just the meal plan alone was a nightmare, as we all know teens eat junk, the poor eat whatever they can get with their Food Stamps, and most of their choices are not good for pregnancy.... oh my, where do I start? I worked diligently on this plan for this child/family for weeks. Just as I was ready to put it into place by going into the home and make a visit to implement it, she left with her boyfriend and went back to Mexico! Okay, now I move on to the next......did I mention that Nursing is a challenging gig?

As I went into the Women's Pavilion and did my clinical rotation through GYN I was assigned a woman who was somewhere in her late thirties. I went in to her for her morning care, and as I was preparing to get her up for a shower I realized she was on total bed rest. Upon reviewing her chart further I realized she had the diagnosis of prolapsed uterus and was about thirty weeks pregnant! I needed to go take a look at this! I went into the room and there, on the bed, between her legs, was the whole lower half of her uterus at near full term gestation. I could easily visualize her cervix and lower section of her uterus. Upon questioning her she said it was totally painless to her as long as she remained in bed. I was shocked, but maintained my calm. I carefully interviewed her and went about my development of a Healthcare plan for her while I attended her. According to her, this was her sixth child, and after her delivery, she would have a hysterectomy. I cared for her carefully and supportively, as this organ was continuously maintained wrapped in warm saline and sterile gauze, positioned on a large sterile pad, we re-dressed it several times a day. When I finished my time on that unit she was still there awaiting the birth of her final child, successfully I hope. As a Nurse you just never stop seeing things that amaze you! It makes you know there is something greater than us managing our universe!

Overall that two years was one of the most educational and exciting times of my life! I learned not only much Nursing knowledge but so very much about myself and my own strength and skills. I also learned of the great inner strength of my family. They missed many prepared dinners, settling for fast food. They went on vacations and weekend trips with a Mother who took textbooks, notes, and study materials to work on while they were at the pool. It was all-consuming! They were, and still are, my heroes!

My children were elementary school age and I recall often, during summer months, dragging them with me to long and boring classes, lectures, and anywhere I needed to go in order to maintain their safety, as I had no babysitter while I continued my own education. I recall my son, age nine, sitting in the back of the lecture hall with me one day and as he was bored, he had put his head down on the desk and fallen asleep. He apparently had a dream that he was at the beach,

a crab pinched his toe, and he shouted out in class, waking from this dream! He was horribly embarrassed and forever remembers this happening and how shocked he was! I guess even though they were captives in the classrooms during their summers, my children learned that getting an education is critical. They now have successful lives and I feel I have earned their respect for working hard and doing what it took to get that education for myself and for them. Later, I would find myself a single Mom and reliant on that education to care for them and provide all they needed.

Nearing the end of our training we found ourselves serving at the State Hospital for the mentally ill. I had never been exposed to what I saw in that facility! We were required by our Nursing Instructor to view a movie that was running currently in the movie theaters. It was about a gentleman who found himself in a local mental institution for behaviors inappropriate to society today. Now to say he was "crazy" was a stretch, as there were many, many other patients within his unit that were without a doubt, and undeniably mentally ill.

He was guilty of just having no "filter" or self-modifying skills in his behaviors. We see this often in very young people who have not had positive guidance in making good choices. Anyway, we were required to view this movie and write a paper about it, determining exactly who was the person, or people, in the movie that were diagnosable. Well, some of the other patients quickly were notable, and easily identified. The main actor certainly had some issues but I could not arrive at an easily determined diagnosis, but someone else really was visibly dysfunctional. It was the Nurse! She was a controlling, inflexible, rude, and non-compassionate Nurse who actually set up the patients under her watch to have melt downs, therefore complicating their therapeutic process. Unfortunately, no one was available in this institution to check and balance this behavior on her part and the ending of this movie saddens me yet today. It did, however, profoundly show us just how Nurses can be therapeutic and support patient successes, or practice in a selfish, non-therapeutic way, with the patient on the losing end of the equation. This assignment was a major learning opportunity for all of us in that class.

We then were delegated to take a small unit of patients in the State Hospital and teach them a healthy, usable skill for their confinement period. Our small study group of seven Student Nurses took on the task of teaching our six patients the game of soccer. We brought a soccer ball, several bright orange cones, and a goal. We took our team outside and set up the playing field and began our lessons. Now, most of us had young children who were learning the game so we felt as though we had this! Well, we had one patient who kicked the soccer ball so hard the ball went over the building and out onto a street, smashed by a city bus! Another of our patients was so obsessed with the cones that he continued to move them all over the area, forgetting about the ball. As a final act, one of our patients, an alcoholic, managed to get away from us and our supervision to cross the street and steal a bottle of liquor from a local liquor store. He was quickly apprehended and returned to his unit. It seems he had done this before. I do not recall our grade on this project but I would not give it anything glowing! We had fun and I think the patients did too, but I am not sure how much they learned or how therapeutic we were for them! I don't think any of our group of seven actually went into psychiatric Nursing after this experience, either.

Finally, in December, 1976 I graduated, with honors, and went to the big city upstate to take State Board Exams for Registered Nursing. Yay! Done...and done! Or am I? We shall see, but done for now! Yay! I was ready to go out there and be the RN that I had prepared for so long. Life is waiting for this "girl" of 32 years!

My husband again had an opportunity to relocate with his job and further develop his career. It was perfect timing for me too. as I was ready to start my new career as an RN!! We had enjoyed a full six years in this town with one of our children in elementary school, and the other entering middle school. We had many friends here with whom we had wonderful memories, but it was time to move on and make new memories in a new town.

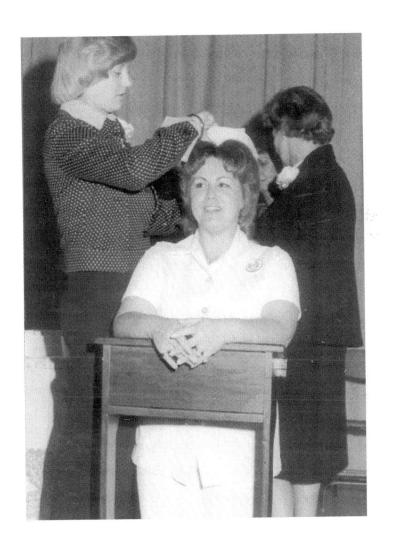

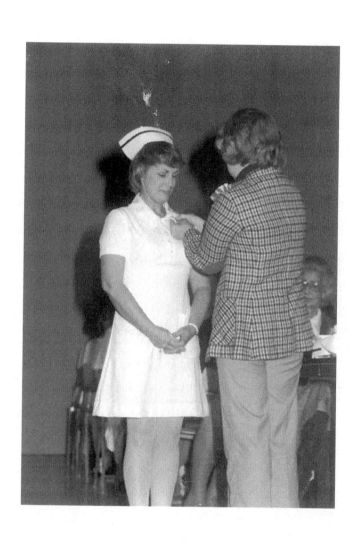

I AM A BIG GIRL RN NOW!!

CHAPTER 16

In December, 1976 off we moved, loading our decorated Christmas tree into the back of the moving van and started our new lives in yet another large city in our state. It was an exciting time for us. After getting the children settled in their local schools, I was off again to get back to my calling.... Nursing! As a new RN I felt that I had the world ahead of me and I wanted to work in the busiest and most challenging birthing unit I could find. I felt that this was my true calling. I wanted to support the birthing process and learn more and more about the complications and challenges of this arena of medicine. My recent three-plus year training had exposed me to all aspects of Nursing but Maternal-Child Health was where I wanted to be!

I applied and was hired at the local Regional Referral Trauma Hospital, a very large teaching hospital in town. My love was Obstetrics and they had plenty of that to go around! I was hired for $5.00 an hour, a fair wage for the year of 1977 for a new graduate RN. I look at this salary now and it is amazingly underpaid, but then again, so was fifty cents an hour for a Nurse Aide. Salaries are certainly not why we go into Nursing, both then and now!

This was the day of the 24 hour hospital day being divided into three shifts, days, evenings, and nights. Most new Nurses are hired to work the night shift of 11PM-7AM, however this Unit had several excellent Nurses who preferred that shift, therefore it was well staffed. I would be working the evening shift, 3-11PM of course..

As Nurses we are flexible and tend to move around the spectrum of shifts as we are needed. In all the hospitals I have worked there is a common denominator. We take care of our patients and our colleagues irregardless of the personal cost. Some of the most moving and challenging events in my medical career happened right there on the "Labor Deck" of this huge teaching hospital.

This was also the time I was raising two teenagers, with a husband who traveled all over the state working and providing a good income for his family. The marriage had barely survived the education piece, we were working hard to re-develop a strong family life again, and trying to dedicate ourselves to our growing children. They were in excellent schools, doing well, we had a beautiful new home built, and things appeared to be good. I was at the right place at the right time, with an opportunity to learn even more before me. I felt that this was my time to spread my wings as a Nurse and become what I had always dreamed of being....a skilled, professional Obstetrical Nurse....a good Nurse!

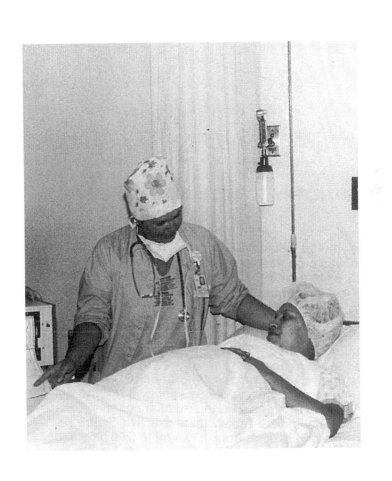

NOW.... THIS IS A LABOR UNIT!!

CHAPTER 17

In this hospital we had residencies in Family Practice and Obstetrics-Gynecology, providing services to all indigent patients in the county and surrounding areas, which also included border towns to Mexico. Every day we welcomed patients from Mexico, patients who spoke near to no English and had experienced absolutely NO prenatal care. Approximately eighty percent of these patients were termed "high risk". We delivered approximately six hundred fifty babies a month, on average, with some months much busier than others. We found that many births occurred during August and September, which are about 40 weeks after the coldest weather in the southern part of our state. We also saw an increase in births about 40 weeks after a hurricane occurred along our coastal area. We actually scheduled more staff on the "deck" during these seasons of anticipated higher birth rates.

Many mothers-to-be made the long trek to our hospital to deliver their children in the USA, hence making their child an American citizen. Most of them were also seeking a safe and healthy place to deliver their young and this was something that I could not feel badly about. That is the only thing a new mother wants, a safe and healthy place to deliver her babies. Many of our patients would give an address of the local T-heads, a dock for boats of all kinds, personal and corporate. When asked to make a co-payment at admission of $1.00 most of them had nothing. They were not denied care and for that I also feel good. No patient should have to go without care based on ability to pay. That was how it was and I loved that. Again, discrimination is NOT a piece of my personal or Nursing world, and I will NOT participate in it. No patient should be treated differently based on race, color, origin, religious belief, funds, or otherwise. In this intense Unit we did not allow any separation of patients based on anything other than medical need. They all received our best care and we saw NO differences. It was NOT tolerated.

When I began there, I did not have any real experience, to mention, as an RN. I was on a huge learning curve and for what I lacked in knowledge and experience, I made up for in eagerness and enthusiasm. I had absolutely no experience in starting IV's short of training on a few rubber arms. Every patient that was admitted for delivery required an IV so that medication could be administered to relieve some of their pain. It also provided an accessible vein for any emergency that might arise.

Remember, the smaller the number, the larger the bore of the needle. The IV needles that we were required to use were a size 18g, and if they were having their 5th or more child, they required a 16g. Patients under the age of 15 or over the age of 40 required 14g, and occasionally we inserted 12g needles for patients at much higher risk. Now this 18g is a really large bore needle and when I first began starting IVs on patients I was actually shaking and nauseous! After about the second week I really began to get the hang of it, actually enjoying the challenge and a skill I mastered proudly.

This was the day of laboring in a bed, then loading the patient onto a stretcher and rushing her back to one of the four delivery rooms in time. We had to call the Nurse Anesthesist, Resident/Intern, Nursery Nurse, quickly put her up in stirrups and ready her for delivery. With all with the timing of a skilled clinician, we welcomed the squalling but healthy newborn into the arms of the Nursery Nurse. This took some practice to get the timing down so that no one had to sit around the cold delivery rooms waiting for the baby to make its arrival. Also, no one wanted to catch a baby on a stretcher moving down the hall. This too, I worked hard at and became skilled and very proud of my ability to get almost everyone there just right and on time. It was critical, especially late at night when the physician had been up all day and was trying to get some much needed sleep.

We rotated through several assigned areas on this unit such as Triage, Observation, Labor & Delivery, Recovery, and Circulating or Scrub Nurse for Caesarean Sections. Each day the Unit Charge Nurse would assign each RN to a rotation of duties throughout the week, making it both a good training exercise for Nurses while providing a variety of tasks to keep it interesting. We were proud to be cross-trained throughout the whole experience of birth. This was considered a Level IV "High Risk" Unit.

Sometime during the six years I worked there one of the Nurses was doing a research class and as a project she collected data and statistics on patient numbers. Her final figures reflected that of the average 650 deliveries each month, the mean average delivery age was 16.3 years old. This was a staggering number in that it indicated that 325 births were to girls 16.3 years old or younger, and 325 births were to girls older than 16.3. My recall of the youngest delivery I ever attended was of a young girl who was 11 years old (of which we had three one year) and the oldest was to a lady who was 57. She was, by the way, having her 17th child.

Our Facility Policy required that she and her husband both agree to sign permission for her to have a sterilization procedure during her Caesarean section, making it impossible to bear further children. He refused. My thoughts have often gone to her and wondered if she had further children in her native Mexico.

As we were a warm coastal town we had a lot of homeless people residing on the beaches in cars. This transient population came to our hospital for delivery. We delivered one of these patients of three children, one per year, for three years in a row. She had Caesarean sections each time and continued to live on the beach in her car. She is another one that I have often worried about. It must be tough recuperating from major surgery, with a newborn, annually, in a car, on a beach. I have to admire the tenacity and tolerance.

We served the jail population, and often we received pregnant patients from both city and county jails. Okay, if you got really tired of sitting in a jail cell and are obviously pregnant, getting a nice outing works if you declare to the jailers that you think you might be going into labor. This will get you a very quick ride to the hospital by ambulance for an assessment. Seldom, nights went by that we did not get such patients, particularly when it was hot and humid in the summer. Jail cells, apparently, are hot, humid, and uncomfortable. Sometimes, these patients were actually in labor and when admitted we were curious, as Nurses, as to what landed them in jail. I guess we just needed to know if they were dangerous, and they received no less care than anyone else seeking medical attention in our facility. It was just the nature of our population.

One of the hardest patients I had to care for was a woman who was carrying twins, in labor, transported from jail, and was charged with neglect and the death of her three year old son. She had locked him in a closet and had starved him, he had become unconscious, and rats had eaten off his toes and fingers. Now I am a very loving and caring, non-judgmental person, and never wavered in my care of patients, no matter their socio-economic status or behaviors. I had to really struggle when admitting, delivering, recovering, and allowing this woman to hold her newborn twin sons. They did go to a foster home and I only pray that they are safe somewhere in a loving home. They would be in their late 20's, just like their deceased brother would be, today.

Another patient that comes to my mind is one of a 17 year old who found herself pregnant, so she and her boyfriend eloped to Mexico to get married. Upon their return to the city, they were involved in a car crash. She was injured seriously, receiving a severe head injury that required surgery to relieve pressure within her brain. Her best friend told the doctors, after the surgery, that she was approximately 8 weeks pregnant. She continued on life support in ICU after surgery and our Nurses went down every four hours, around the clock, and monitored the fetus until she completed 34 weeks gestation. The senior GYN resident came up one morning and said she was mature enough for delivery and he wanted to do a Caesarean section right away. She was still on life support, essentially functioning as an incubator growing a fetus for twenty six more weeks. She was quickly delivered of a very frail infant with microcephaly (having an unusually small head and brain), hopelessly handicapped for life. My last knowledge of this family was that the father left and joined the military, never to be seen again, the little Mother was being cared for in a long term care facility, and the infant was being cared for by grandparents. So is the life in a teaching hospital....one of seeking the best possible outcome for the patient, irregardless of situation. This was a very sad but wonderful learning opportunity for everyone involved in this case. Teaching hospitals teach everyone who walk through the doors!

Late one afternoon we received a call from the Emergency Room downstairs to send down an experienced High-Risk Nurse from our unit for an emergency delivery. Now, we had been called down regularly and on many occasions to deliver a baby in a car, the ambulance bay, in the back of trucks, and in any other variety of modes of transportation to the large hospital. Nothing surprised us, so as usual I grabbed the Emergency Pack and off I went!

Upon arriving I was directed into a trauma room where a woman lay flat on the table, her hip-length blonde hair hanging down off the table into a floor soaked in blood. The Intern was feverishly working on a newborn lying on a table behind her, administering CPR to the lifeless little child. The young Mother was obviously deceased, having had an emergency evacuation of the child from her full-term uterus, and now they were working to save the infant. After about twenty minutes it was obvious that the child was not going to make it and they ceased working on him too, and both were pronounced.

After collecting our thoughts and de-briefing, we received the information from the local Police Department that this Mother-to-be was on the back of a motorcycle that had crashed. She was thrown into a curb, was briefly unconscious, but came into the hospital talking and providing information, appearing somewhat stable. Suddenly she began to bleed from her nose, mouth, and ears, and had apparently suffered a ruptured aorta and bled out in minutes before anything could be done to assist her. We also discovered that she was actually full term, with no prenatal care, and had asked for a ride home from a bar with another customer that she did not actually know. Unfortunately, her little baby boy did not have a say in the way he was being transported nor what was to happen to him before he even had the opportunity to live his life. He was, however, perfectly formed and quite a handsome child, never to enjoy his world.

While working on this unit we had, in addition to the Interns & Residents working in the teaching hospital aspect, several private physicians that had practiced in the city for many years. They brought their private patients there, as most of them were at poverty level and these physicians chose to deliver there. They knew their patients would be treated well and their hospital bill would be handled in a much kinder way than in a private facility. As discussed earlier, the sheer volume of patients was stressful, the level of care required was extensive, and our Nurses were stretched beyond belief. We seldom had enough staff to fully manage the constant flow of patients arriving or to provide overnight care to patients who were not impending delivery status.

We had one of these private physician who, no matter how busy we were, no matter how many patients we were currently caring for, or how highly critical any or all of our patients were, her patients were ALWAYS admitted. We had standing orders to admit her patients upon arrival, feed them a light meal, provide them a shower and fresh gown, and let sleep until she came to make rounds the next morning early. When we were short Nurses, delivering several babies at the same time, admitting actively laboring patients one right after another, and doing back-to-back surgeries, the last thing we needed was a sleeping patient who was NOT in labor! These patients still required the standard of care of vital signs and fetal monitoring on a regular basis, and observation. We could NOT just put them to bed and ignore them.

After a particularly busy night, we received two of her patients late in the evening hours on a hot summer night. With the usual need for more Nurses on deck, we had followed her standing orders, and done the best we could to provide an acceptable standard of care to her ladies. The next morning she arrived at her usual early hour and proceeded to discharge her patients, who had slept all night. I sat down with her and in an exasperated but kind mood I asked her, "Dr. ★★★★, why, on a night that we are so very busy, short Nurses, and stretched to the limit, do we have to admit your patients who are clearly and evidently NOT in labor?" She patiently looked at me and smiled and said, "You know, and I know, based on your fine judgment, they are not in labor, but have you thought about what they really need? They do not need a labor Nurse, but perhaps just a place that has air conditioning, as they do not have that in their little home…..and a nice fresh light meal, as they have had to cook and serve everyone all day at their little home…..and a quiet, secure, safe place to lie down and get a good night's sleep, as they are likely in a house with many noisy people, lots of little ones to care for, and too many people in their own bed to get a good night's sleep. They are near delivery time, overweight and miserable, in their pregnancy that they likely did not plan, and just need some love and attention. They come here because THEY NEED SOMETHING FROM US….. and we need to provide that to them." I thought for a minute and suddenly understood. I gave her a big hug and a bigger smile, and told her that I understood! We need to listen, as Nurses, and hear their needs. No, they did not need a Labor Nurse but just a kind person who can give them a smile, provide them with a cool room, clean sheets, peace and quiet, a light meal we have delivered to them, and a good night's sleep.

This woman was an old wise Physician with a much broader vision for patients that we were missing. As a young Nurse, I grew that moment. I shared it with the Nursing Team at report and it made a major difference in our concept of what was important and what was urgent. All patients need what we have to give and each one is different and special. Thanks to this kindly Physician we all grew as a team, both in compassion and skills.

Another day, this Physician shared with us her payment policies in her office. She said she ALWAYS made the patients pay for their prenatal care and delivery. Now, knowing her kind heart, we had to wonder why this would be her policy. She explained that it was about pride and self-respect. When the patient came for her first visit the Physician told her that she MUST pay something. They had nothing, but they must pay. The patient and she discussed what they could afford and that was what they paid. Some patients paid with a chicken each visit, some brought tamales, some tomatoes or other fruits or vegetables, some mowed her lawn, some cleaned her car or house, but everyone paid something. Dr. ★★★★ said that in her many, many years of caring for maternity patients, she had ALWAYS gotten paid something, and she felt valued, while the patient and family maintained their dignity and self-respect. This Physician was wise and loving, and somehow teaching us her values. What a gift!!

It was not uncommon to receive anywhere between fifteen to twenty new patients to triage and observe, every shift. Elevators were just outside our triage rooms, with easy access from downstairs ER directly to the labor deck. Orderlies and aides were often seen rushing out of the elevator pushing a patient in a wheelchair in active labor, near delivery, with big eyes…..the orderly had big eyes, not the patient! Their greatest fear was to get caught in an elevator delivering a baby! Also, frequently we would receive a patient from ER who had delivered at home.

We assisted many deliveries in the actual ER, as the patient would arrive too late to try and get upstairs. We "dug in" down there and delivered in an exam room. We had a phone on "the deck" we referred to the "bat phone" which was a direct line to the ER operator. If that phone rang, the unit secretary answered it, as the Nurse assigned to emergency responses would go for the emergency delivery tray and head down the back stairs. We maintained an incubator downstairs over in a corner, warmed and ready with an emergency delivery tray sitting on top. This was in the event we had a precipitous, emergency birth downstairs, and of course, we frequently did. We had a plan, and we were good!

One evening I walked out to triage and as the elevator door opened a small, pale girl walked out with a bundle in her arms wrapped in a soiled bathroom mat. A newborn infant was howling from inside this wrapping. The girl was barefooted, crying, and dangling between her legs was the severed end of the umbilical cord. I immediately got her on a bed, clamped the baby's cord stump, the dangling cord end, wrapped the baby in warm blankets, and prepared the girl for a trip to a delivery room. Upon interviewing her, as we prepared her with an IV, lab work, a clean hospital gown, and loving comforting words, she told her story. She explained that she was home alone and had prepared to take a bath, felt her bag of water rupture and run down her legs, and had one or two contractions, dropped to the floor, and delivered a beautiful lusty, crying baby girl. She had nothing to wrap the baby in but the bathroom mat. As she was alone, and lived only two blocks behind the hospital, she simply cuddled up her baby and walked those two blocks to the hospital.

This is an amazingly brave and strong act , however, that is what I learned as I worked with these patients on a daily basis.....they were tough beyond belief! I fear that I, personally, could NEVER have been able to do what this young girl had done. However, we don't know what we are capable of when we are desperately in need, alone, and are providing care for our young! I always felt that I must teach and lead them, as patients, but I often felt that I learned more from my patients than they from me!

As this was a busy, ever-evolving patient unit, we performed Caesarean sections almost back-to-back. One of our private surgeons was very vocal, and often spoke in a foreign language rather than English, his second language. He consistently swore and yelled at Nurses, Scrub Technicians, and anyone around him if things did not go just as he thought they should go. He did not get the idea that this was a unit that delivered multitudes of babies per month, and crisis care was an on-going process.

I was the assigned circulating Nurse for one of his Caesarean sections one night and that means that I am in charge of all "counts" of sponges and instruments. The mandatory counts occur several times throughout the case while the patient's abdomen is open. If the counts are not accurate at any time the case stops until it can be righted and everything accounted for. He was performing a tubal ligation too, and had removed portions of the fallopian tubes. I halted the case because the sponge count was missing a single sponge. He began to yell and curse in his foreign tongue and refused to stop the case, as I again reported that the sponge count was incorrect and he could not proceed until it was correct. He continued to close the surgical wound. I then walked to the doorway to report to my supervisor that I needed our Chief of OB to contact me in OR immediately. As I turned my back I felt something hit me in the back. I turned and this surgeon had thrown two instruments with the portions of the fallopian tubes across the room and struck me in the back. Well now, this was a whole new thing......being hit with body parts during surgery.

As you well might guess I did complete my mission of reaching our Chief of OB who immediately came to the room, relieved that surgeon, and completed the surgery for the patient. He then followed up by removing that physician from his services on staff for a specific period of time. He also was severely chastised for his inappropriate behavior on duty. I also received a written and verbal apology for his immature behavior. I was somewhat amused at how these medically skilled men can act when performing some of the most important care necessary for another human being. It was sad but amusing and has made for some interesting event-sharing throughout my years of story-telling. I continued to work side by side with that same physician for several more years and he showed me respect for my profession, and I returned the same for his. We all experience lapses in judgment, and it is certainly forgivable. It is what it is.... stressful!

Another day a young woman was in labor and her very anxious and sensitive husband was nearby. She advanced to the point that she was nearing delivery and he became more and more obviously nervous, pacing in and out of the unit. When the obstetrical resident examined her he decided it was time to "rupture her membranes", as this would help her progress on to delivery more quickly. This was a common practice and very safe for both mother and infant. When he had completed this, he and I walked out to the hallway and found this nervous father-to-be. As I stood next to him the physician gently told him that we had done this procedure and why. This young man became extremely agitated and in the flash of a second swung his fist toward me and struck the wall. I could feel the breeze next to my cheek as he launched into this tirade, saying, "Oh my goodness, you have done what!? You have ruptured our membranes!? How dare you!?"

He then proceeded to drop to the floor, curled into a fetal position, wailing and screaming his wife's name, and security was called. He apparently was not mentally stable and the stress of the day was too much for him. I was visibly shaken that I had come so close to being struck! My heart broke for this man who, due to his meltdown had missed the birth of his first child. He was taken to the ER, sedated, and admitted to the Psychiatric Unit hospital for observation and treatment. I could not take it personally, as it had nothing to do with me directly, and I felt only empathy for someone who was overwhelmed by the momentous event occurring in his life. We take care of everyone. That is what we do.

Another event on this unit occurred one evening while I was on duty in Triage. We received a call from the ER that a patient who had delivered at home was heading to our unit, so I met the Paramedics at the elevator. On the stretcher was a little girl, no older than 15, who was awake and alert dressed in tight jeans and a shirt, and at her feet was a tightly wrapped and covered bundle. Upon report from the ambulance team, the bundled infant was deceased and the little girl was not talking about it. Shortly after, a pair of city detectives arrived and after we had gotten the patient settled in a bed, in a gown, with her IV flowing, allowed them in to talk with her. I was asked to stay as her chaperone as she had no family with her. Her story followed.

She was knowingly pregnant, and had shared this with her boyfriend of 16. They chose to just ignore the fact and she went about her life, going to school, participating in gym, and doing what 15 year old girls do in 9th grade. Apparently she snugged her tummy well enough that no one, not even her parents, realized she was carrying a growing baby in her surprisingly flat tummy. She went into labor during the night, her membranes ruptured, and she delivered a full term little boy in her bedroom. He cried, she cut the umbilical cord with a pair of scissors and wrapped him up. He continued to cry, and being afraid that he would wake her family, she wrapped him up and took him outside to the family camper and laid him on the bed. Now, even in the south on the coast, winters are humid and cold. That winter night temperature was below forty degrees, certainly not warm enough to meet and maintain a newborn's necessary temperature needs. Sadly, sometime during the night he succumbed to exposure. The next morning the young girl got up, dressed and went to school. When her boyfriend drove her home they had decided to pick up the baby and take him to a local charity for adoption. They retrieved the child, arrived at the office of the charity and the secretary noticed that the child was not breathing. She immediately called 911 and both mother and baby were transported to our facility. The detectives determined that there was no crime, other than lack of knowledge, that caused this infant's death and it fell upon us to contact the girl's parents to come to the hospital. No charges were filed. We took her to the delivery room, treated her post-delivery condition, and she was admitted for a few days for care. She was oblivious to the infant and appeared to be totally uninterested and disconnected to this child she had delivered.

I went home that night, sat my own daughter down, who was also 15, and had a long conversation about what had transpired that day, with name confidentiality, and assured her that I would be available anytime she needed to discuss anything she needed. I have to wonder where the communication was in this family, when a pregnancy could come to term without the knowledge of parents..... but it can, and did. We can only hope to make certain it does not happen in our home with our own teens. In the months and years to come my sweet daughter had to endure many conversations like this one, as I did not want to see her experience what I saw daily at work, naturally. She was very tolerant of my ongoing reminders and cautionary talks.

In this city we had a large community of motorcycle gang members. It was a large, practicing, land-owning, business-owning, drug-dealing, gun-carrying group. They were certainly intimidating on the freeway, riding in packs of 10-15 on loud motorcycles and looking dangerous. It was my experience that they did not typically bother the everyday citizen in the community, but rather mostly conducted their sordid and illegal activities on the street and were dealt with by law enforcement as necessary. Also, seldom did we deliver their babies. For whatever reason, they did not have many babies.

On one occasion I did have the opportunity to labor one of their women, and as I arrived in her room she was laboring totally unclothed. She chose to labor without the gown or sheet over her and I must say it was a bit shocking in the beginning. She had a tattoo that was a HUGE eagle and his beautifully done feathered body covered the whole front of her torso. His wings extended out over both her arms, inside and out, and his talons were wrapped around a large tattooed snake that was coming out of her belly button. Now in a dim labor room this is quite the sight! I immediately saw, and visualized, a large bird writhing around in the bed! Fortunately, she was not in labor long and she and her eagle were soon in recovery room, cuddling a small baby in their arms/wings. My first and my last of the motorcycle babies, and I just could not help wondering how this baby was going to straddle that big bike!

That motorcycle gang was usually parked as a large group in the parking lot outside the ER, particularly on Saturday nights. I worked the late shifts and often walked out the ER door, as it was the only one unlocked at that late hour. In the beginning I was a bit frightened walking past or near this group of people however, I must say that after a while, I never felt safer. They would tip their well worn variety of caps, hats, or bandanas and speak to me in a very gentlemanly way, with respect and kindness. They were simply waiting for an ill or injured comrade who was likely being seen in the

ER. After a number of years I actually felt secure walking through that otherwise deserted area. As they gathered there in the parking lot, standing guard, of sorts, for all of the Nurses leaving or arriving late to duty, they felt good. I developed a respect for them as people irregardless of their less than savory activities.

I had been told at one time, "Nurses and Nuns….safe in any environment"! We are seen as the good and loving, trusted people we represent in a society that has little trust for those around them. I like to believe that, and as I have continued to practice my Nursing skills throughout the years I like to think we are the ones anyone can trust, and they seem to.

The other side of that is REALITY, and drugs and alcohol have taken that common trust and judgment from society, so we are not as safe as we once were. We now have to be practical and sensible. Again, Nursing comes from inside the heart and even knowing this real danger I still would NOT hesitate a minute to provide anyone, under any conditions, with my best Nursing care under any circumstances. That is what a good Nurse does!

Now, shortly after my fifth year at this hospital we had a huge grain elevator explosion in our coastal city. It was a grain storage facility near the harbor where grain is shipped to other countries, and is stored as it awaits loading into cargo ships. We got the call overhead that we, in the hospital, were in a "CODE BLUE" status which meant emergency crisis mode. It was declared when we were in hurricane preparedness mode, tornado alert, or civil or other crisis situation in the city. When the explosion occurred, all emergency vehicles were activated to the site, all law enforcement personnel activated, and of course both hospitals were put on alert to receive incoming patients. Being the largest as well as the best staffed local teaching hospital, we were to receive the most severe and largest volume of patients.

The call came at about 4PM on a weekday when I was leaving after my day duty shift. Doors slammed shut and the operator overhead announced that no one was to leave their duty stations. If getting off duty, like our day shift team, we were to report to the

Emergency Department immediately to support incoming patients. The other Nurses and I went right down to the ER and made ourselves available. I quickly stated, "If someone is having a baby we are your girls, but otherwise we are willing but not highly trained in explosions."

We were put into the triage room to start IV's and monitor vital signs while the multitude of physicians triaged and routed patients based on medical need. I do not recall how many were lost that day but we were able to contribute to their need in the ER willingly and tirelessly. There were burns, explosive wounds, and shock. It was certainly outside the comfort zone of several Obstetrical Nurses, but we were good at IV's and sterile technique. Nursing is Nursing. We left there sometime just after midnight and were tired but self-fulfilled and content. It felt good to be a Nurse! Little did I know what was right around the corner.....a Nursing enemy!

Sometime around that time after working several double shifts, staying late, coming into work early, and experiencing a sixteen day run without a day off due to staffing shortages, I let it slip up on me......Burn-out!! All of a sudden, like darkness, it consumed me. I did not want to get up and go to work. I wanted to just stay in bed and never see another patient. I literally became nauseous when arriving at work. I was grumpy, tired, mean-spirited to my family and friends, and saw no way out of this darkness. I took a few days off here and there, but it would not go away. I considered resigning and to go to work doing something mindless.....I was done! This caregiver's bucket was empty.

My listless marriage was floundering, my teenagers were making some questionable choices, and I had no idea what I would do or where I would go if I was not a Nurse. It would appear that I had reached my limit. I took the night shift just for something different, and slept long days. I declined extra shifts, staying late, and ignored phone calls for help on my days off. I went from Clinical Manager of the day shift to Staff Nurse on night shift. Soon, the circadian rhythm of working nights and sleeping days took its toll on me too. Done....and done!

I wrote my resignation several times, but did not submit it, as I needed to work for the income, and had few other options. I knew I needed a change but did not know what or how to make it happen. After praying about it, and long, sleepless days and nights filled with deep thoughts, I finally turned in my letter of resignation. I had made a decision. I could no longer be a Nurse. It had taken my heart and soul, my spirit was broken, and my body was tired....at the age of 38, I was done with Nursing.

All I could do was go through the Grieving Process, one that I was well trained in by now.....Denial, Anger, Bargaining, Depression, Acceptance....and hope to see some light at the end of the tunnel. I had grieved many things, deaths of infants, adult patients, my children and their choices, my dying marriage, and so many other losses, but the loss of my Nursing career was a whole new challenge. This was my life and it defined me. I was not me without being a Nurse. It was like the loss of a long known loved one. I circled through this process sometimes hourly, sometimes daily, but kept circling it. I felt trapped. Who would I be if I were not a Nurse? It felt as though I had hit a wall and I seriously did not know what path I was taking.

Little did I know that right down the road was the answer. My husband was taking a business district further north, so we would sell our home and move again. Then I would consider what I would do. My daughter graduated from High School, my son was about to enter high school, and we were on the move again. This was a good thing!

....ON THE ROAD AGAIN!!

CHAPTER 18

After seven years on this labor unit, even with the current feelings of burn-out, I still felt very skilled. I had seen and done many things, had experienced more than most Nurses had in a lifetime of Nursing. It was time to move on. My husband had assumed a new region of the state, and we were relocating there. My daughter was entering the local university after graduating from high school, my son was preparing for high school, and actually eager to attend a different high school in another town. He was always ready for a new adventure and making new friends. It was a good time for all of us to make a move.

I spent several days and weeks searching for a new home in the new area, about three hours away. We found a beautiful home and learned that a new hospital would be opening soon in another small town nearby. My husband's work would be out of a large nearby city however, we were ready for a smaller town to live in. We decided to locate about an hour out of the big city. Schools were good, commute was easy. Small town life always had agreed with us as a family. After getting settled in our new home, I began to feel that old pull to the bedside again and the urge to care for patients. After considerable thinking, enjoying the changes in my life, and getting some much needed rest I secured a position in a new little satellite hospital. I started a new chapter in my Nursing life at this little new hospital.

I was hired to work on the Labor, Delivery, Post Partum, and Nursery unit of this tiny 120 bed hospital. WOW!! What a change for me! I had no idea how it would be changing. First of all, new hospital and doctors, and second of all, new Nurses developing into a new working team. I welcomed the challenge and met it with my usual enthusiasm! I was entering a new chapter in my life and Nursing career, and up for the change! It is just what I needed for that old burn-out!! I had beaten it! It was actually exhilarating to get a brand new start with a totally new group of Nurses coming from a variety of backgrounds. Time to power up again! I began to feel that old enthusiasm come over me and ready me for a new tomorrow!

It was exciting with unpacking, setting up, and getting this brand new hospital into working order before the first patient arrived. We sterilized supplies, set up patient rooms, made beds, set up the nursery, stocked the labor and delivery areas, and made sure everything was just right. We worked on Policy & Procedure Manuals, developed orders cards from our physicians, and labeled everything, everywhere. We practiced all aspects of the hospital-provided birth process, trained new staff, and felt that we were a good team ready to meet this new challenge!

Then we waited......and on the first week we opened, all of our OB doctors induced their patients who were ready for delivery, and we had sixteen babies in one week! It was hectic, noisy, worrisome, chaotic, stressful, but successful overall. Gosh, I had done that in one hour at my last hospital! We celebrated the first baby born in the new hospital with gifts and joy! We also learned that we still had a lot to learn.....specifics for each doctor, more specific supplies not considered earlier, special instruments requested by certain physicians, and just learning to work with each other as a team was a big challenge. We were up for it! There were, of course, many fewer of us than I was accustomed to work with on a shift, with only two Nurses per shift, plus a Nursery Nurse, provided we had a baby in our nursery......so it was a BIG change for me. I was accustomed to having fifteen to twenty Nurses on duty on the labor deck, and eight to ten Nurses in the nursery, with two in those busy recovery rooms. We did not even have a recovery room! The patients labored in one of the two labor rooms, delivered in the one delivery room, and recovered back in their labor room. In the event of a Caesarean section they went to the operating room, then to the recovery room attached to the operative suite, and back to their room in post partum. Quite the difference from what I was accustomed to on that big labor deck in a teaching hospital.

We even performed epidural anesthesia in this hospital for patients in labor! Getting doctors to our deliveries from their offices across the street, or across town, and not just from another area of the hospital was a big learning curve for us. Timing was critical for all aspects of this new environment and we all learned well. We became family.

After a year of this we averaged approximately fifty babies per month. This was far removed from the six hundred fifty I was accustomed to, but it was a great change for me, and I enjoyed it. We often worked extra shifts for one another, relieved each other on back-to-back twelve hour shifts, stayed over to support a busy shift, and everyone respected and appreciated each other. Our Director of OB-GYN, a seasoned Nurse, was a joy to work with and we all cared about our new unit. We saw patients from very affluent areas of town, as well as seasonal migrant workers who came to our hospital in desperate times for them. I was very accustomed to these indigent care patients and was able to welcome them along with anyone else who arrived to deliver their precious cargo. We worked for very energetic and caring doctors who were willing to work with us on whatever we needed, as both experienced and new Nurses worked on this new team.

One night I was caring for a laboring patient, a beautiful girl who had shared that she was a dancer in a "Gentleman's Club" in the nearby big city. This lovely girl was married, having her first child and was quite the trooper while in labor. She planned on an epidural for her anesthesia for birth, so as she arrived at the appropriate level for my calling in the anesthesiologist we made the call. He arrived and as she turned over and sat up, she had the most beautiful "trellis" of yellow roses starting from her lower sacrum to her neck, and about six inches wide.....all the way up her back! My Anesthesiologist took one look at this lovely tattoo and immediately explained to her that she could NOT have an epidural placed in her back, due to this tattoo. It was not safe to administer epidural needles through this inked marvel. I was disappointed for her, and she was certainly disheartened. I immediately got orders and we made her otherwise comfortable with some IV sedation, and she went on to have a relatively comfortable and successful delivery. Okay, so now I have learned something new! NO spinal tattoos for when I might need an epidural for something later in life…..no problem here!

Another memorable event while working at this small but efficient hospital was of a gynecological nature. We admitted, prepared, and cared for, post-operatively all women's surgeries such as hysterectomies, D&C's, and tubal ligations. As it was Women's Care, we felt more qualified to provide their care and patients would receive the best of care within the Post Partum unit under our treatment.

Early one morning we admitted a nice middle-aged lady for scheduled surgery. As I sat in her room and got all the paperwork done I sensed the smell of alcohol strongly. I continued her admission process and at some point asked what she had eaten or drank during the past twelve hours. She smiled cheerfully and said that she and her husband had gone to dinner the evening before and when they arrived home had drank about two bottles of good wine, somewhere around midnight. She had understood that the "cut-off" was midnight so she polished her bottle off by midnight. I had lab draw a blood alcohol along with all her routine labs, and it was well beyond the legal limit to drive, however she assured me that her husband had driven her to the hospital so all was well, right? I did not think so! I submitted the lab results to anesthesia and the physician and anesthesiologist immediately came to her room, cancelled her surgery, scheduled her for a week later, and she was sent home to sleep it off. Anesthesia and alcohol are not a good combination in the OR! She was upset but learned a valuable lesson herself on that one!

Another day we delivered a patient from one of the Pacific Islands and moved her over to the Post Partum area for a few restful days before going home with her newborn. Upon arrival into their room most patients are eager to get a shower and wash their hair. They seize this time to get refreshed, spend some time with their newborn, and then settle in for a nice long restful nap. This patient immediately sent the baby to the nursery and went to sleep. I asked her if she would like to take a shower and get freshened up and she looked at me horrified! She said "Oh no! I could NOT get into water so soon after delivery, I could die"! I sat down to talk with her about this fear and she explained that in her country, custom is that you do not take a bath or shower for up to a week after delivery, or you can become gravely ill, or die. I did not force anything on her, particularly when it comes to custom and beliefs, but instead gave her a small basin to wash her face and hands, to brush her teeth, and gently refreshed her, otherwise, myself.

Later, I asked a fellow Nurse about this who had lived in the Islands for awhile, and she gently explained to me the story behind it. First of all, in some countries, water supply is from the local river, not treated, and more often than not, very contaminated. Now, just imagine giving birth, then going down to the river and taking your "bath" in that water. Of course you would risk becoming very sick, as the pathogens and contaminants floating in dirty river water would enter the body from the damaged birth area, and all sorts of illness could ensue. Common sense in their world, not even considered in ours......so her caution is based on facts, and she is protecting herself.

After two days she went home and I suspect did just fine. We are so set in our own cultural routines that many times we forget lessons learned in places we can only imagine. We have always felt secure to climb into a nice warm tub of tap water and soak, without the dangers she had seen visited on her friends and countrymen. She, again, had taught me something....and we are always learning!

While working at this hospital, I celebrated my 40th birthday. I felt it was a measurable milestone in my life. I had learned and experienced so much, was very blessed in my life, and had achieved my dream of being the best Obstetrical Nurse I could possibly be. I had worked hard, trained long and hard, dedicated myself to my chosen career, and even though I felt "half-way done" on that day, somehow I felt I had also just begun. I hear forty is the new thirty?

As for the burn-out issue, I have often discussed it with fellow Nurses, and we have come to a general agreement. First of all, take care of the caretakers before it hits. When we get a day off, relish it, spend quality time doing what we want, make short trips to local towns of interest, shopping, a little partying at local watering holes, lunches out, and just "refilling our own buckets." It is a realization that if we do not take care of us, no one else will. I take better care of myself today, as best I can!

A NEW BEGINNING!!

CHAPTER 19

About this time in my life, I realized that my marriage of twenty one years was winding down. We had grown apart and were not enjoying life together anymore. Our kids were growing up, one in college and one in high school. We, as a couple, seldom spent time together and when we did it was no longer enjoyable. We had nothing in common in our lives but the almost grown children, and they were all about their own friends and lives. One night, I sat them down and talked with them at length about my thoughts, concerns, ideas, and options, and they understood and agreed. My then-husband and I had already talked about it, and knew it was just the end of this part of our lives, and certainly the beginning of the next new chapter in our lives. We all knew what we needed to do to move forward in our lives....all of us. The kids were understanding and supportive of both of us.

My husband of twenty plus years and I decided to end our marriage. We would remain friends throughout the rest of our lives, enjoying family gatherings at the marriages of our children, births of grandchildren, and holidays. As the extended family grew, we celebrated their graduations, athletic events, and birthdays, sharing them generously. No animosity, just a civilized agreement to go our separate ways and enjoy the rest of our lives, eventually, both of us, with someone else of our choosing.

I found a small home to rent nearby, and we obtained a quiet, peaceful divorce. Both children were okay with this and I felt good that I had a career to rely on to support myself. Our oldest child was out and on her own in college, our son was nearing high school graduation, and the kids and I settled into the small cozy little house in a quiet neighborhood in this same small town. This small hospital I worked in was supportive, loving, and became an extended family during this time of change for me. I took on extra hospital shifts to make extra money to sustain myself and our needs after the move. Eventually, I wanted and needed the opportunity to make more money, and broaden my skills. Our home had sold, my son had graduated and moved into the bigger city, so it was time for me to make a new life for myself in another place. Not far away, just in another environment. It was time to move and grow again.

I still loved what I did, saw opportunities that would be greater, more challenging and exciting in the city, so I decided to move from the small bedroom community to the larger town nearby with greater Nursing opportunities available to me. I restarted my career at a two hundred fifty bed hospital in this town, and chose to work the midnight shift, as it afforded a much higher salary and more freedom and opportunity for my personal life.

I worked from 11 at night to 8 in the morning, and began training to become a "second assistant" for emergency Caesarean sections. This meant that I would work evenings and stay in-house to be available for assisting surgeons in emergency surgeries during the night. This meant they did not have to call in an assisting surgeon late at night. This was quite exciting for me, as I was well versed in attending Caesareans from my days in the teaching hospital. I worked evenings on the unit, then would go to the Nurse lounge and sleep in my scrubs, only to be awakened during the night by the RN on duty to assist, or at 7AM to go home off duty. I loved this!

My son graduated from high school that year, and my daughter married. I enjoyed the challenge of learning new skills in a field I loved, again made wonderful Nurse friends, and worked with some of the brightest and most dedicated medical team members of a lifetime. Nurses seem to become family without a thought, just become family. Overall, it was an eventful and productive year.

Somewhere along the way, that year, I met my soul mate. I met a man who was a Viet Nam veteran, and a very colorful fellow! We began dating, and he was always in awe of the fact that I was a Nurse. He has a strong respect for Nursing, and he tells me often how proud he is of me for the profession I practice.

He says he was often "put back together" by Nurses, hence his love for us? He spoke kindly and lovingly of the endurance and resilience of the Nurses that served in combat hospitals during that horrific war. He had an undying respect for those ladies, and often told me of how they could not take time to sit and play cards or have something to drink, called 'down time.' They never seemed to get a break from the vicious combat and related injuries that were horrifying to everyone. They just kept receiving injured soldier after injured soldier, never ending, and unrelenting. They treated these wounded warriors with loving kindness and patience. He felt they suffered much more in combat than the soldiers did, as they were often under fire and not always well protected.

In fact, in a downtown Veterans Day parade he joined, he was carrying the memorial wreath to lay on the capitol grounds one year, and upon arrival, he handed it to the Military Nurse walking next to him to place. He said she had earned that privilege more than he had. I know she still likely remembers that gesture, and appreciated it so much.

Unsung heroes! Nurses wear many uniforms, and our military sisters are to be honored and revered. We have seen nothing compared to what they have endured. Bless them!

After a year, we married in the tiny chapel at the local Air Force Base. It was a small wedding, attended by my family. It was a good choice, this man of mine, and I have never regretted it. He is my greatest supporter, loudest cheerleader, and no matter how long my shift, workdays in a row, late hours, or how tired I am, he is my greatest support person for my Nursing career.

He has driven me to work on days or nights that the weather was treacherous, and picked me up after an exhausting shift of his own. He has brought food to the unit for a team of hard-working

Nurses that he had cooked all day, knowing that we were busy and not taking time to eat. He has come to the hospital just before my shift ended on snowy days, scraped the snow off my car windows, warmed up my car, and left....so I would have a warm, clear way home after a long day on the unit. He has listened to me cry, laugh, scream, agonize, and anguish over about everything one can think of, who works in Nursing. He has stayed up all night and waited for me to get off a twelve hour night shift. When I finally came home, we have slept all day together, only to have to go to work himself in the afternoon. I have always appreciated his candid views and loving support, and I cannot appreciate him enough.

Along the way, we have seen my children marry, and grand children born. We have supported and loved them, them being there for us when we needed them. He has taken good care of this Nurse, and her family! How much does this man get it? Let's see....

AN ADVENTURE OF A LIFETIME!!

CHAPTER 20

After our marriage, we decided to take a huge leap of faith, and as I had always wanted to live in the beautiful state of Colorado, we moved north! We chose a city and packed everything up, loaded the dogs, and off we went on an adventure of a lifetime! We arrived in our city in winter, and found an absolute wonderland around us. It was exciting to just take off, like pioneers, and move to a place where we knew no one, but with a career in Nursing, anyone can do that!

We arrived, and within days, after finding a house to rent, I was hired at a local Birth Center based on my diverse background and experience. Nursing jobs are universal! I was at work within a week, barely unpacked, and certainly not knowing my way around town. Our adventure had begun! My husband found work quickly, and with us both working, we realized our risky plan would work. It was exhilarating and somewhat melancholic.....leaving my grown kids, everything and everyone behind, to venture into this whole new life!

Snows came, with us undaunted by the daily driving, and we enjoyed this whole new environment that we were in....but I missed my children horribly. I had not really thought it would be that hard on me, and the days at work filled the lonely hours, but everywhere we went, I found myself wishing I could share the experience with both of them, and the first grandchild. Before long, our son had joined us to work & live in our new adventure, and my daughter and grandson came for a visit with us, which made it all better. It made it easier, even though I longed for my family, I knew we could do this, and if we did not, we would regret it someday. Weekends and days off were precious to us as we made day trips all over the state to experience this beautiful exciting new life of ours. Nursing was quite different at this new altitude, but I loved working and living here. Now, to settle in for this adventure of a lifetime!

Colorado is well known for its high altitude....the question, whether one has oxygen or not, is the motto here! This is something that I had a quick lesson in. When we arrived here, it took about three months for us to adapt to the lower oxygen content in the air. We had intervals of "sparklies" and feeling faint and tired when we walked up stairs. It was a struggle to unload the moving truck....even our little dog would lie around a lot and seem to feel tired! Finally, we were transplanted....we could climb stairs, walk uphill, and not suffer from altitude weakness! We were full-on Coloradoans!

Now, Nursing is certainly different at this altitude too! Mothers on obstetrical units in the southern state had bigger babies, more often suffered the complication of pre-eclampsia or eclampsia, or high blood pressure of pregnancy. They seldom delivered small, underweight, or premature babies. High altitude mothers experience smaller babies overall. They experience a higher risk of pre-term delivery, based on dehydration and lower oxygen concentrations in the local atmosphere. As I learned more about the high-risk aspect of mother-baby care here, I realized that simple geography and climate can cause a huge impact on both, depending on where they live. I was highly experienced in caring for mothers delivering big babies, at sea level, with pre-eclampsia partly due to elevated salt in the atmosphere, and foods grown and diets eaten. This new environment taught me how to care for this new population. I became comfortable with administering more medications and IV's to stop labor, and the details of managing pre-term deliveries of small babies. It was challenging, but rewarding, and certainly taught me the other side of high risk pregnancy, labor, and delivery. I can never stop learning as a Nurse, and this was a huge learning curve for me, but I adapted to it and loved what I did!

This local Birth Center delivered about one hundred fifty babies per month, which was just like the nursery rhyme about the three bears, just right! I worked with many skilled Nurses and Doctors, learned much, and was able to utilize my past experiences daily. By this time in hospital staffing, shifts had evolved to 12 hours. Staff worked 7AM-7PM, and 7PM to 7AM. I liked that schedule, working both shifts, per diem as needed, since it allows staff to work only three days a week with four days off, and we were paid for 40 hours! Eventually it began to require an eight hour shift somewhere during the two weeks to equal a full 40 hour week. Still not too bad!

After a year of this schedule, a position opened for a Day Shift Coordinator, and I applied, and got it. It required a five day week of 8 hour days, Monday through Friday. It also had a higher salary. It involved scheduling about forty Nurses for the Birth Center per day, and an on-call schedule to be responsible for. I still got my "fix" of delivering babies, my first love, when I filled in for staff on busy days or when someone was ill or absent. It was busy, and I was privileged to work with some of the most talented Doctors and Nurses I had ever had the pleasure to meet. Many of these Nurses were married to military men and had served in the military themselves, and were amazing Nurses. I learned much from them, and the teamwork was always there. Everyone had each other's back, and our love of Nursing bonded us. In my small office was an oblong cardboard box. Inside was a handmade infant coffin. Now most people might find that odd, but a Nurse is ready for anything! As a woodworking hobby, one of our custodians made infant coffins, out of gratitude to his church. He lined them with soft, silky fabric, and made them very beautiful. He donated them to various funeral homes, or people in need when they suffered the loss of an infant. He had donated this one to our unit, and it had been in my office for about two years. We made room for it and respected the duty it was to be called to. We all knew it was there, and it remained a constant reminder of what we did....taking care of patients in need.

One rainy afternoon, we had a patient arrive in our triage room in labor, and she and her husband had two small little boys with them. It was a rapid delivery, and during the hectic preparations she stated that she and her small family had just come from the airport, and were new arrivals from Ireland. They had packed all they owned into suitcases and sold everything else, bought plane tickets for themselves, and had come to America to start their life all over. I suspected that the flight over had precipitated her labor and delivery, about three weeks early. Unfortunately, at birth, the beautiful little baby boy was stillborn.

It was a sad welcome to our wonderful country, so we Nurses gathered together and put this family at the top of our priority list. We arranged for a small home for them to occupy for free, owned by one of the Nurses. We collected money and food for them, clothing and toys for the boys, and I called a well known local funeral home and arranged for a brief but dignified memorial service for this lost new child, at no cost to this struggling family. I told them I even had a coffin for the infant to be buried in. The problem we had was that, according to state laws, the funeral staff could come to the hospital and pick up the infant, but not the coffin. I quickly made a phone call to my husband, and he immediately hopped into his SUV and came and picked up the small coffin in the box, in pouring rain, and delivered it to the funeral home.

We spoke with the hospital administration, they quickly placed the medical costs into the "needy" category, and just like that, we had a family who could go to a comfortable place to grieve and heal, and be met with open arms into a country that welcomes all to our shores. We arranged for follow up visits by our hospital social services, to see that these sorrowful folks had what they needed after discharge. I have often thought of this little family and hope that we were able to meet their basic needs in a time of stress. That is what good Nurses do, Right?

I worked holidays, weekends, odd shifts, and often when I myself was ill, just to make sure we had coverage. I worked with a physician who I was certain was going to be hit in traffic as he dashed across the busy street outside to arrive just in time to greet a newborn. We survived on popcorn and odds and ends stashed in the Nurse lounge, as we seldom had opportunity to actually stop, sit down, and eat a meal. Such is the life of a busy Nurse on a busy unit. Patients were kind, brought us boxes of candy after delivery, and we hungrily gobbled it up as quickly as it was opened, shared with our sisters on duty!

One day I came on duty and a patient was about ready for delivery, and her physician was standing beside her bed as she pushed. Each time she pushed, she screamed loudly. Now, I frown on this behavior, and I have coached many ladies through this phase of labor and delivery without any of us screaming. It is a horrible waste of energy, and robs the unborn baby of much needed oxygen. Besides, it is unnerving, frightening and disturbing to other patients and families in the unit. I walked into the room, just as she let out a loud howl. At her feet, her doctor, who was a dry comedian of sorts, was howling with her! I said, "What is going on in here?" He quickly said, "Well, I am screaming with her so she won't feel like she is behaving inappropriately"! I immediately began kindly coaching her, and laughingly shushed him, and said, "You know, both of you are behaving inappropriately.....and I won't have it!" They both stopped screaming, she pushed, and out came a beautiful pink baby! You can't make this stuff up.....and you just have to laugh....right?!

One very busy afternoon a patient arrived and was in active labor. She stated that she had previously had three Caesarean sections, so we immediately went into overdrive to get her ready for another. We notified her physician, got permits signed, started her IV, shaved her tummy, placed a Foley catheter in her, and got a quick fetal monitor strip run on her. She was all ready to go, and when the team from OR came for her off they went! I had done most of her preparation, and after she left, I happened to look down, and my ½ carat Princess-cut diamond from my wedding set was missing! I rushed over to the OR and thankfully, they had not changed the sheets on her gurney in preparation to bring her to recovery! I looked under the disposable pad, there it was! My diamond from my ring!! I have never been so happy in my life! I could not believe that I found it after all that chaos. I guess my very weary guardian angel was still there…looking out for me!

One afternoon we got a cell phone call from one of our physicians. Now, this is a Doctor who sauntered everywhere he went, put his cigar on the edge of our Nurse station(!!), which we quickly snuffed and disposed of, and wandered into the birthing room of his patient. Often, we "caught" his babies, and we did not mind, as we were highly trained and experienced in this type action. He would just walk softly into the room, nod his head, slowly gown and glove up, do his part of the final exam, pat the Mom on the head, with a "Good job, Mommy". He then would shake hands with the Dad, and offer a hearty but earnest "Congratulations, Daddy", and give us a pat on the back and mumble something about "Nurses 1 – Doctors 0", and wander out in search of his lost cigar.

Now, back to the story….I do digress……anyway, we got this call and he said he was enroute to the hospital with a patient. Surprised, we immediately set up for an emergency delivery, and after some time, he arrived. He had stopped at every red light on the way, and observed all the laws of the road while bringing this fortunate lady with him to the Birth Center. His office was about ten miles from our hospital.

It seems that she had arrived at his office, sat down, and failed to mention to his office staff that she was in labor. While waiting, her water broke, and she went into the waiting room restroom there to take care of herself, again, without calling any attention to anyone in his office. While in the restroom, she felt the urge to push, delivered a healthy, lusty baby, and someone heard it crying, and called for one of his Nurses. She was immediately assisted back to the exam room, and as the Doctor was about to come to the Birth Center to check on another patient, he just her put into his SUV and proceeded to the hospital with her and her lusty, healthy newborn baby. Upon arrival, apparently as she stepped out of the vehicle, she expelled her afterbirth on the sidewalk, he picked it up and assisted her into the waiting wheelchair, and in they all came. I met them in the hallway and with shock and dismay, immediately took the newborn to the nursery warmer, and we got her into bed.

Thankfully, she was an experienced birthing mother, her newborn was healthy and strong, and she was in excellent hands....her NEW doctor. Yes, this was her first prenatal visit, at full term, and her job was done! Afterwards, as he completed his mountain of paperwork, we had to discern a birth time, for both the baby and the afterbirth, give the baby an APGAR rating, and he said to us..... "you know, my staff is excellent and they kept a cool head, and I don't mind giving this girl a ride to the hospital, even if my car is now a mess. What I am most disturbed by is the fact that she pulled the towel rack right off the wall in our office restroom during this delivery. Now we have to have our handy man come and repair that, and try and match that wallpaper in there!" I find this Doctor confident, unshaken, solid, and still retaining his sense of humor. How many Doctors do you know that would have driven a patient who had delivered in their office, to the hospital? I also understood from his staff that she had no insurance, so I am more than certain that he was considering the fact that an ambulance ride would have been way too expensive for this lady. He was the type that would think of that, and that is how a Doctor should work, right? What a gentle, loving man who just simply takes care of others. You cannot make this stuff up! Life as a Nurse is full of surprises and giggles, tears and stress, and every bit worth it, everyday!!

Back in the late 1980's the infant seat laws came to be. Our Birth Center had a policy that when a new baby went home with its family, we were to see it put into a car seat and latched in, legally and safely. We actually signed a form stating that we safely buckled in the infant in a way that met state law. That included having seatbelts in the seat that worked, and strapped to hold the infant seat in correctly and securely.

One snowy day I discharged a little family, and there were several family members there in celebration of this new baby in their large family. They chugged the old car up to the curb, as I stood inside the door with Mama in her wheelchair, holding her precious bundle. We always waited until the last minute to roll them out, so the family all piled out of the car and began the process of locating the seat belts within the old car, for the hospital-borrowed infant seat they were using. They searched and searched, finally one older man went to his old beat up truck across the parking lot, got a tool box. The men began to dismantle the whole back seat, finally got it out, and sat it on the curb. There were the seatbelts, beneath the seat, on the floor of the old car, old and unused all these years. They finally managed to get the belts out and up, placed the back seat back into the car, and got the belts through the back and into their proper placement. They then began to attach and strap the child safety seat in effectively. This whole event took about forty five-minutes, during which Mom did a short breast feeding, burping, and changing in the hallway. Finally, the baby was bundled up, placed in the infant seat, strapped in tightly and snugly, and was ready to go. Off they chugged to their home, and who knows what......but that baby was safe on our watch!! It was strapped in tightly for the journey home.

During my years at this hospital, Nurses came and went. Nurses are as migratory as birds, always willing to go somewhere else and do something else exciting. We were holding interviews for Birth Center Nurses and as I interviewed them with my Administrator, one who applied was a man. Well now, that was surprising. I had worked for many years in a teaching hospital and was surrounded by Interns and Residents, mostly male, and they were all over the Birthing Unit. This hospital, being a religion based private hospital just might not consider a male Nurse a good candidate for the Birth Unit. He brought many years of experience from another state, had excellent references, and was a mature, clean cut, well educated Nurse.

I convinced Administration to take a chance with him, and when it was announced at our staff meeting, Nurses were fine with it, however a few physicians were not. Some of them did not want him caring for their patients, as they felt he would make them uncomfortable. The physicians that welcomed him were pleasantly surprised and validated that their patients, upon being questioned after delivery, loved his gentle and caring Nurse. The physicians that denied him never changed. A few patients who returned in a few years to deliver again actually asked for him! He was definitely a loving and caring Nurse to add to our team, and irregardless of gender, patients saw him as a wonderful Nurse who cared for them during birth.

One evening I was on duty with a great Nurse whose husband was a pilot for a local USAF base. I overheard her conversation on the phone with him about nine PM one night. He was apparently experiencing some difficulty getting their two little boys, ages three and five, into a bath and to bed. Now, I had had some of these same conversations and issues in the past years of my working this evening shift too with my own children at home. She said, "Honey, I cannot believe that you can take off, fly, and land F-15 and F-16 jets safely, but cannot get two small boys into a bathtub, bathed, and into pajamas for bed." I just chuckled.....Nurses are beautiful!

After about six years of this hospital assignment, as you might now realize, I am beginning to get old! As a matter of fact, I had turned 46....and to some, that does not seem so old, but I felt old! Yes, I had become weary of long days and nights on shift, working holidays and weekends, and just the stressful duties of hospital Nursing, overall. I resigned from this position I had held for so long, and began to explore my other options. Something less stressful, and for me, healthier would be in order about now. Teaching Nursing, maybe??

I decided I wanted to go back to school and get my BSN. I realized that is a must if a Nurse is moving up to another plane of Nursing, such as teaching. I have always LOVED school, and of course, that interested me, so I began to look into schools.

My sweet husband was a Veteran and unable to use his education grants provided by the military endowment, but he could pass it to me, his spouse, so we went down, checked on it, and got it going. I enrolled into a local BSN program that allowed me to work if I wanted to, and get my Bachelor's degree in two years. It was one of the most exciting educational times of my life! I felt that I was learning things I had needed all along, and would certainly use in my Nursing career. I wanted to gain a higher education, work part time, and prepare myself for Nursing on a higher level, which would be kinder to my physical health and process of growing older and wiser. I needed to do this! You are never too old to go back to school!

We lived "out in the country", with bad weather and distance working as barriers to frequent trips into town. In Colorado the mountains are beautiful, and we certainly were in a beautiful, but somewhat isolated area. As we aged, and struggled to manage our life out there, we realized we had some thinking and planning to do for our future. After shopping around and determining where we would fare best, we built a beautiful new home in town. Now we had access to wherever, whenever we needed it, and were safe and secure. We felt it was time to move forward in my education, and being in the city was a big part of that decision process. Okay, another adventure......!

BACK TO SCHOOL......AND WORK!!

CHAPTER 21

About this time, a friend of mine was teaching at the local Community College, and suggested that I teach a class or two there. I was looking for part time work as I took classes toward my degree. They were always looking for Adjunct Faculty to fill in and teach a class here and there, she said. I applied, interviewed, and was immediately hired for teaching a Medical Assisting class.

Medical Assistants were a new breed of health assistant that works in medical offices. Physicians were beginning to utilize them, and the local Community College would develop a program to appropriately train them for this profession. Win....win! Now, as usual, I was clueless as to what a Medical Assistant does, or how to train them, so I began to self-learn what I needed to know. If nothing else, my Dad had taught me to keep myself informed, as it was my duty! I would inform myself of this task at hand and move forward....Nursing school did not prepare me for this career choice, so I would go out there and just figure it out!

I got myself a corner office, a computer, a desk, and in the middle of the clinical lab classroom, I made my debut at teaching! I taught first year students the finer skills of working in a medical office. Now, if you recall, I had a lot of experience in working in an office as a LVN, and knew what the job was like, so off I went with it. I had the textbook, put together lesson plans, wrote tests and test keys, and prepared laboratory practical assignments. It was fun! Maybe this teaching thing is where I need to be! I taught students, mostly adults, and some newly graduated high school students, day classes, some night classes, and the occasional Saturday class. I continued for a year as Adjunct, and was finally invited to be a full-time staff member and Department Chair for Medical Assisting for the college. This was exciting and challenging, but I knew I could do it! I did some teaching, some advising into the program, and a lot of paperwork. I wrote curriculum, developed new courses, scheduled classes in the bulletin, and taught some more classes. Advising was great....leading people into a career that I felt promising and enduring, re-inventing lives, and offering encouragement to new and old students alike! All this I did while attending night classes for my BSN.

That first year of teaching at the college, I suddenly lost my sweet Father to a long term illness. I received the call early one morning, and within hours, I had notified the school, and one of my fellow Nurses stepped right up. She not only volunteered to cover my classes for the week, but also arranged complimentary airfare for me through her husband, a pilot for a local airline, and I was on my way. What a blessing from a newly made friend, and a living example of how Nurses step up and take care of their own sisterhood. It made that loss so much more bearable, and I never forgot her for it. That is what Nurses do, we take care of our own, and everyone else in the meantime.....Thank You again, my Good Friend....you know who you are!

I felt a connection to most of my students, but one in particular, a single Mom, who sat in the rear of my class and wept as I taught the electrical firing mechanism of the heart. She was usually the most enthusiastic and energetic student in class, and at break, I asked her if she was okay. She quietly explained that several years ago, while carrying her one and only child, her husband had suddenly passed away from an undiagnosed electrical malfunction of his heart. He was a healthy, robust, active soldier with a lifetime ahead of him to enjoy his family....suddenly gone from her! All I could do was listen and hope to empathize with her as to how she must have felt. I certainly could not say, "I know how you feel", because I don't. I have not ever suffered that kind of loss in my own life. I also had to continue to teach this aspect of the function of the heart, and was sorry it was such a sensitive area for her. This is the part of Nursing that is the empathy we all feel at given times. We can feel the pain someone else feels only through our own eyes, not their own, however we must feel their pain. That is what gives us the aspect of Nursing that allows us to step out of our own skin and into theirs, and understand.

I still know this student today, and she has gone on to become one of the most dedicated and skilled Registered Nurses I know. We are still friends and co-workers after all these years! Bonds are made every day, and some to last a lifetime. I cherish her today as one of my dearest friends....and now, much respected colleague!

We had labs on designated days, and the students' family members came in often to volunteer for injections, blood draws, electrocardiograms, and a variety of practices necessary to train for working in a physician's office. Some students brought in whole platoons of soldiers, as a service act on their part, and students "practiced" on them....wrapping limbs with ace bandages, changing dressings, testing blood glucose levels, and performing a variety of other procedures, to prepare these students for the workplace. We had the occasional fainting student during these labs, some sweating and paleness of the skin, and a little throwing up here and there, but overall, everyone seemed well suited for the career they had chosen.

I enjoyed teaching at this college for six more years. The Nursing Program, along with several programs, relocated to a new building at the opposite end of our large town, so the commute was exhausting and frustrating, but I continued to drive miles and miles, no matter the weather. I saw many students come and go, found them sites in medical offices all over town, oversaw their clinical experiences there, counseled them in life choices, career choices, and family choices like a good advisor.

During that first year I also grew. I completed my Bachelor's Degree in Nursing, my BSN! Upon completing it, I realized that I had achieved something valuable and powerful. We walked graduation, had a grand party to celebrate, and now I would teach and see what comes next for me. Nursing is ever-changing!

Some of my students went on to Nursing school, as they had the diligence, dedication, and perseverance that is required to stay that course, my widowed friend being the strongest I know. She is my proudest moment of those students.....she has done it through persistence, aguish, and dedication. Her path has not been easy, but she is here! Others work today in medical offices, having achieved their idea of what they want to do as a career, and still others found work in other career fields for whatever reasons. Hey, Nursing and healthcare is NOT for everyone. The important thing is to know that and seek your own dreams and successes. For us, we are living our dreams!

I listened to many interesting papers presented about non-traditional medicine, acupuncture, historic medical practices, and a variety of topics that would be a part of the larger picture of medical practices today. In one of my classes, a student was living here for a year, native to an Asian country, to learn more about "western medicine". She was going back to her native country to blend the two into her own medical practice there, with her physician husband. I have thought of her often and wonder if she has integrated what we taught her into her eastern medicine. We surely learned much from her about that culture and their centuries of medical practices.

I had students who married, gestated their first child, and almost delivered their babies in my classroom. Many of them struggled to continue their education in order to provide for their families. The dedication and intensity that some of them exhibited was so very inspirational to me, and I learned as much from them as they learned from me. They worked one and two jobs, attended classes at night, most were single parents, and often were very tired and sleepy on days the classroom was warm and quiet. They often had little gas or needed tires for their old raggedy cars, but they chugged along, and it made that final class and graduation so very special to them!

I attended graduation services every May in the large auditorium in town, even being honored by speaking at one. I was asked to deliver one single point that I would like to share with families and friends gathered for the celebration of graduating from our college, a first in some families. My message was simple....I learned something every day from students, as I taught them lessons in healthcare. I learned patience, family supporting family, endurance, and the ongoing need to improve one's life, and its importance. These students gave me much more than I was able to give them. We Nurses never stop growing! They inspired me to continue my own education.....nothing is impossible, nor unrewarding!

I realized that I did not miss bedside Nursing at this time, as I felt I had evolved into someone who could move into a teaching role. During that first year, I attended meetings, sat on committees, led groups, advised students, and forged ahead with faculty meetings and curriculum. I still felt that something was missing. Soon, my Dean came to me, after the first year, and announced to me that without a Master's Degree in Nursing, I could not continue to teach at the college. They wanted me to get that higher degree. Now, you have to recall that up until now, a Bachelor's degree in Nursing was not a common education level. It was considered a higher level of learning, with a Master's Degree in Nursing almost unheard of. I had been considering this step all along, and knew it was a good move for me both personally and career-wise. I could do this! I would go back to school....yet again....and continue my education. I had grown children, so how hard could it be? Besides, I was just finishing my Bachelor's and was still in a pretty good study mode!

OFF TO COLLEGE.....WELL, SORT OF....ONE FINAL TIME?!!

CHAPTER 22

In this day and time, 1995, one does not pack her bags, load her car, and head off to college, at the ripe old age of fifty! Actually, most students these days take the non-traditional approach and attend classes online, or classes one night per week, and cover a lot of material online, or in that four hour class once weekly. As an adult, assuming my adult education classes, I chose the latter. I could not see myself doing all my studies on the computer, as Nurses traditionally do not usually have a natural "computer gene" necessary for that. I wanted to actually sit in a class, with a professor up front teaching, validating, confirming, and correcting. I need that type feedback, and was willing to do the work between weekly classes to bring what I needed to class and share. It had worked well for my BSN. It worked perfectly for me, as I was still teaching during the day at the local Community College.

I met with advisors at the big local University and determined that all my current ADN and BSN transcripts would, in fact, transfer. I did lack some classes at a higher level, such as Fine Arts. I immediately decided that I did not have the time to sit in classes all day, but once a week at night, I could do.

I had a job ahead of me! I also discovered that I could challenge and test out of certain classes.....for which I did. I tested out of a 400 level Abnormal Psychology and a 400 level Math (Horrible....but got some tutoring from a colleague at the college). Now for the last of the prerequisites necessary, and I could be on my way to attaining my MSN.

My own advisor at the college shared with me that I needed to add a Fine Arts class at a 400 level to my transcripts, so I determined that that Fine Art needed to be something I could relate to in Nursing. After some further discussions and advisor approvals, I decided on Philosophy. I searched and searched for local classes, online courses, and nothing would fit my work and college schedule, and I could not take it locally, as there were no classes at a 400 level in our town, taught when I was free to attend.

I would have to go to a neighboring town, forty miles south, and the opportunity of class there was mid-day. I arranged my teaching schedule for mornings and afternoons, leaving me free to travel south over a two hour "break" between classes, twice weekly, rain or snow, for the Fall semester. I would enter a four block study of 400 level Ancient Philosophy, at the fourth level, and get my Fine Art completed. With this plan in place, I thought I was all set. Well, now, was I in for a big surprise!

I registered, paid the tuition, bought my textbook, and drove down the first day of class at noon, and arrived in the classroom on time. The professor was dressed…...well, let's just say he was dressed like a Philosopher. He had on rope sandals, a very loose hemp shirt, and appeared to have parked his "hippie van" just outside. There were a total of six students in his class when I arrived. They all appeared to know him well, having discussions about their previous three blocks of study under his tutoring. They were all equally casually dressed, while I had arrived in my appropriate teaching attire, which was professional in nature. He immediately turned and looked at me, and walked toward me, saying, "And just who are you?" I told him my name, and he asked why I was coming into his classroom during the FOURTH block, having NOT attended or passed any of the previous blocks. I assured him that the Registrar had approved my attendance, as I was a 400 level student. I explained that I needed a Fine Art, and I felt that Philosophy would be the best suited to me, as I could perhaps relate it to my health education and career. He openly glared at me, indicated my seat to take in his classroom, and said to me outright, "Well, I certainly appreciate your intentions, however, having no background at all in the study of Ancient Philosophy, I seriously doubt that you will be anywhere near successful in passing my class. I will, however, indulge you and not dismiss you immediately from my room." Well now, my Daddy did not raise a shy girl, and I professionally, but forwardly, replied to him, "Well, I certainly appreciate your candor, Sir, and I can assure you that I will be your most studious and hardworking student. My plan is to take this class, learn all you have to offer, study my hardest, and earn a good grade in your class." He had no idea that my whole MSN program hinged upon my getting this class completed by December, so that I could begin my Advanced Nursing Clinicals in January. I had my work cut out for me, and I knew I would do whatever it took to succeed.

This class was hard! I studied a lot, read a lot, and prepared for every class, attending all of them. I learned of Saint Tomas Aquinas, Plato, and all the ancients, trying to relate them to Nursing, and actually found myself enjoying the information. Being somewhat of a history buff, I really did like what I was hearing and learning. This professor was a tough taskmaster, and passionate about his lectures and beliefs. We learned of men exiled because of their religious beliefs, executions based on race or religion, and social atrocities far removed from anything I had ever heard of.

Finally, the end of the semester was near, and as he always tested us with discussion questions, we were told of the five questions we would be elaborating on for the final exam. We would choose three of the five and write three pages on each of those. Now discussion, I can do! I chose to be the over-achiever that my Daddy had raised, so I studied ALL FIVE! I was prepared to discuss, at length, all five of his topics. I attended study sessions with my small but intense class, in the library, taking one of my own precious days off to do so. I was going to be very ready, and up to this challenge!

I arrived in class, sat down with sharpened pencils, and was ready for this final! He proceeded to write five totally different discussion topics on the board. He turned and said to us, "Nothing is guaranteed in life.....here are your five topics on the board, so choose two and I want a page each." Everyone was horrified, and being the girl my Daddy raised, I had re-read and briefly studied all of my notes for the semester. I wrote a page for each topic I chose, and turned in my final exam. Now remember, this has to be a transferrable grade for me to get into my Graduate Clinicals in January! I did not know what grade I had going into the final exam, as per his "philosophy", so it was anyone's game! I just gave it my all!

Two weeks later my grades arrived in the mail while I was at work. My husband called and asked if he could open them and let me know what I had been anxiously awaiting, and I said "Yes"! I had gotten a C......now, for me, an A-B student, this was a huge disappointment! I did, however, rejoice in the fact that anything from a C upward is a transferrable credit! Yay! I passed his class! I was set to graduate, after completing Advanced Clinicals, with my Master's of Science in Nursing! This class held the whole key to completion of that degree! It was exciting that I had met the challenge and could, with a lot of study and hard work, pass a class that I was challenged with on the first day. Score one for the old lady!

Life went on, and one afternoon about a week later, my husband got a phone call from my professor, and he wanted to talk with me.....I was at work.....so he told my husband to give me the message that he had made an error in his grading, and had transposed some grades inaccurately, and that I would be getting a grade change..... that I had actually gotten a B in the class, and that he was sorry for the mistake. My husband called me, and I again rejoiced! I had done better than I had ever dreamed I would! Score another one for the old lady!

January arrived and I began my next leg of the journey to my MSN....Advanced Nursing Clinicals and the courses required to support them. We attended classes every Thursday night for five hours on campus, so every Thursday I stopped there rather than coming home for dinner. I studied, continued preparing for delivery of papers, gathered data in the library, and wrote papers in APA format while waiting for class to begin. I would attend class, get home late, and be at the Community College to teach an early class first thing in the morning.

Now, you have to understand that there were about fifteen other MSN candidates, working Nurses like myself, who were on the same journey I was on. We made a dedicated and supportive team. We worked all day and studied all night. I was thankful that I had only a husband to neglect, and not children.

If I can make any suggestions at all to anyone planning to pursue a Nursing (or any other college prep) career, please do so before you have children, or even a husband, therefore you will not have anyone to neglect! They will appreciate it! Please, get that education done and in the "bank" before making life commitments and having to juggle so many important people and things. Be good to them, and yourselves....educate first!

I completed classes in Healthcare Budget & Finance, Ethics of a variety of topics, Human Pathophysiology, College Algebra, and too many other subjects to recall. We worked in small groups of two to four, presented papers, discussed pros and cons of medical articles and current Healthcare issues. Finally, we neared the end of this leg of the journey. We could see the light at the end of the tunnel!

We performed our actual clinicals at an administrative level in local Nursing Homes, visited homeless shelters and camps, and volunteered in indigent clinics. When I made the decision to stay overnight in a homeless shelter to get the vision of what it truly was like to be homeless, my husband put his foot down. No, I would not be subjecting myself to the dangerous environment of a homeless shelter now or ever. My clinical partner and I settled for spending the day there helping with food, laundry, and did some child care for respite for the clients there. It still gave me a good idea of what these unfortunate people were enduring. It was a time of self exploration and gratitude for what I have, and daily take for granted. There is so very much out there for us to learn!

The only class I ever was absent from was one at the end of a day that I had to attend an all day meeting at the large town, well north of our city. It was one of those meetings that went all day, and I was exhausted at the end. I thought I must be coming down with something. I stopped at a gas station and changed clothes for class, something more comfortable, and as I drove south, I became very ill. I finally felt so bad, I pulled in to a rest area and put my seat back for a short rest. When I woke up, some hour or so later, it was raining hard, and I had five minutes to get twenty miles further south, to get to class. I stopped twice more at bathrooms on the way, and when I passed the exit to get off for class, I just nodded and headed home. I was at home for several days, violently ill, with a visit to the hospital for an IV for hydration before I could get back on my feet. This bug had laid me low! I got my first B in that class, for the night I missed, as I was not there to discuss my latest medical article, but I was fine with that.

One of our more amusing professors was our Algebra Instructor. He came into the room on the first night, we Nurses were all just sitting there waiting for him, all with our smiles upside down! Now, you have to realize something....Nurses, by the majority, are not interested in Math! We are not wired for math equations and all those objective signs. We are more "touchy-feely" by nature. This is the class we had all been dreading, and made no false impression that we were in any way interested, just commanded. We all introduced ourselves, he introduced himself, and we were off and running. His first statement to us was, "I know you hate Math....I get that.... so, just imagine my job right now! The only thing worse than you having to learn this Math, is that I have to teach you Nurses this Math. Let's get that out right now in the open!" He chuckled, and we dove in. I have to say, he made the Math class tolerable, and even for a bunch of Nurses, we almost enjoyed it! He was a good sport, and we gave him our best, and a good time was almost had by all! College Algebra....done, and done!

We students became a tight group, with only about fifteen in our class, and graduation was a celebration, with friends and family. We celebrated with a big dinner and dance in a local Convention Center, with music, food, and drink. It was a wonderful feeling of completion....again. This class included mostly women of my own age, and we were all working as Nurses already, so it was a wonderful celebration of a step up in the right direction. We all had grown children, and grandchildren by now, and it was a proud moment. MSN...done and done....Yay!

MY OLD ENEMY IS BACK!!

CHAPTER 23

I continued to teach at the college for about two more years, and then that old demon….burn-out….came around the corner again! I had just completed, non-stop, a three year college run, had lost my Mother just at the end of that, was stressed and overloaded with student advising, teaching five or six days a week, and supervising some Nursing Clinicals on weekends. Shame on me! When do I learn? I suspect I was not filling my own bucket again, and as no one else was either, the inevitable happened. Suddenly, we lost a beloved little dog, and that put me over the edge. I was down, and could not get up!

I had already considered that I would seek something different before this family tragedy, on the heels of the loss of a parent, but this did it for me. I was done….put a fork in me….I was out of there! It was the end of term, and a good place to step off the runaway train that I felt I was riding. It was an easy decision, and I felt no guilt. Nurses always get up, brush themselves off, and get back in the game. That is who we are, and I was no different. I just needed a "timeout"…..so I took one!

For several weeks during that summer, I languished around the house and searched my mind for exactly what I wanted to do. I knew that I needed to put this education to work, for no reason other than it was valuable and I had worked hard for it, hence it needed to be put out there. Depression and restlessness set in and I did not have any idea which way to go. I have a busy personality, and I need to keep up and out, and sitting around licking wounds was not my style. I just needed to find another niche to fit into where I could be the Nurse I knew I could be.

I sought a great counselor and we explored where I was emotionally and career-wise, she taught me how to refill my bucket, and I spent several months healing and re-energizing.

I baked a lot of bread, read a lot of inconsequential books, sat on my deck in the sun, took naps, and I guess, getting really good at this re-energizing thing after all these years, I managed to heal and prepare to go back.

All that I had done, I guess, was a great choice. One day I found myself ready to get back in the game! Thanks to this supportive professional counselor, I was once again myself, with a full bucket, and ready to go out and serve as I was trained to do. Thank you M'am!.....

THE WORST....AND SHORTEST..... CAREER CHOICE IN MY LIFE!!

CHAPTER 24

One afternoon, after reading the local newspaper for classified ads for Nursing jobs, I saw an ad for a local women's clinic that we have all heard about. They are frequently plagued with demonstrators and protesters. They wanted a Registered Nurse for only a few days a week. I called, set up an interview, and thought finally, I can put my women's healthcare back to work here....they do counseling on birth control, women's health exams, and some good work for the population I enjoy. Right? Now, I knew they did procedures that I was not altogether comfortable with, but I naively thought that I could choose what I would be doing, and not those things that I was not agreeable to. Okay, what was I thinking?

Well, at the interview, I learned that they were hoping to train the right RN in ultrasound, counseling, and overall women's health. They made a salary quote (not critical to me), potential schedule (only 3 days a week), and a job offer to me. I accepted and went home to prepare for a whole new career start....hopefully one where I could make a difference in the lives of young women. This is going to be good! I was hopeful that I would be able to pick and choose......

I arrived on my start date, ready to go to work. I was immediately assigned to IV starts and observation of ultrasounds performed on patients who were at a variety of stages of their pregnancies, and were scheduled for terminations. Wait! I am not certain I am really right for this one! Terminations....not mentioned during my interview!

Okay, so I started the IV's, pushed the pain and loss of memory medications, and got the patients ready, after ultrasound confirmation of gestational age, for the procedure. I watched the ultrasounds, observing movements of the little immature fetus, and then followed the patient into the procedure room, the termination, and on into the recovery suite. Wow! Not what I signed up for! Whoa! This is totally the astral opposite of what I have spent my whole Nursing career doing! Delivering live babies versus termination of small, immature developing fetus'....this is well outside my own comfort zone, for sure! I suddenly realized that in order to work for this organization, one has to be comfortable with everything they do.... and I am NOT their girl!

At the end of the day, I met with the supervisor of the clinic, and shared my feelings with her. She was kind and patient, but assured me that I would be training very soon in the aspect of ultrasound for these patients. She reminded me that I was a valuable and highly qualified candidate for what she had in mind for me, and was looking forward to my expertise in this clinic. That is all well and good, however, I must feel I, personally, can carry on in this environment. Okay, I will return tomorrow and give it another try. Let's just see how it goes....

I returned for the next two days, with every day going home and wrestling with my ethics, heart, and emotions, crying, praying and asking for guidance, and not certain if I could manage to continue on this path. I had several sleepless nights, struggled with actually dressing and getting into the car and going to work, and just cried a lot overall, throughout every day and evening. Now, it has been my experience, if you actually have to almost hold a gun to your own head to get up and go to work, something is definitely NOT RIGHT! Nurses MUST be true to themselves!

I felt that I could perhaps make a difference in this aspect of Nursing. I really did want to give this a chance to work. There were a variety of ages and situations in the patients we saw in this clinic. There were very young, unmarried, high school girls, middle age, married and unmarried women, and older women experiencing unplanned pregnancies. They were a variety of race, age, marital status, and economical situations….all with a commonality of unplanned pregnancies, and an unwillingness to continue to carry the fetus to term. They wanted to end the pregnancy and go on with their lives. Okay, their choice, right?

It was assuring that this choice was being supported in a healthy, safe environment with medical support and emotional counseling at hand. It just was more than I was willing to deal with personally. I have to say that the care was good. Left with no other options, these ladies were usually making a painful and well thought out decision about their own bodies and lives. I thought about the other options women had, historically, for many years, of the back alley butchers, and contaminated, untrained and unskilled abortionists that provided this same service to unfortunate patients. Many of those patients were victims of infection, hemorrhage, and loss of life. At NO time could this decision be taken lightly by anyone, and I was thankful that these ladies' needs today were being both medically and emotionally met at this clinic. I just CANNOT be a part of this aspect of medicine. I am not the girl for this job!

At the end of the first week (three days), I went to the supervisor and told her that this job is not for me. I cannot continue to attend terminations, and I accept that some of these may need to occur, for a variety of reasons, however, I cannot, in good conscience, attend them. I thanked her for her offering of the opportunity, but I would not be returning next week.

I went home and agonized and prayed for days and weeks, asking forgiveness for the role I had played in this experience, and the small lives that I had seen sacrificed in the name of "family planning." It took me several weeks of sleeplessness, personal agony, crying, thoughtful contemplation, and frequent prayers asking for personal forgiveness to get to a place where I felt forgiven and whole again. I realized that I went into this job very emotionally fragile to start, and it was just too volatile for me to continue. I guess everything we do is a learning opportunity, and I was powerfully assured that this is not a part of medicine that I am comfortable with. Forgiven, I move on....

I do remember, many years ago, in a Psychology class, writing a paper on my thoughts on termination of pregnancy. We observed clinically, as Nursing students, in a clinic similar to this one, and it was emotional. In my youthful wisdom, even then, I took the stand that abortion is a necessary procedure in some situations, but as a means of birth control or family planning, not an option. There are so many better ways to accomplish that, and ending a life is not for me. I am certain, like prostitution, homelessness, panhandling, and other societal issues we face, this issue is NOT going away, and has been with us for centuries......and will remain with us. I just choose NOT to be a part of it. I finally feel forgiven.

This was, by far, the worst career choice I have made, to date, and am a better person for experiencing it, however, I know I made the absolute right decision to distance myself from this part of Nursing. I cannot be a part of ending life. I cannot be a part of the whole process of the mass loss of lives performed every day in this arena of medicine.

I will find myself and something that I can do that is validating to both myself and my own personal ethics. I know something is out there that will bring me the satisfaction and growth that I need at this point in my life. I will take my time and I trust that something fulfilling will come my way. I just have to be willing to sit and wait it out. I have a loving and supportive husband and family, and a wonderful education, so I will sit on my deck in the sunshine and wait it out!

I pray often for those little lost lives, sacrificed daily for a variety of reasons. I feel forgiven, however, for my part in it and continue my journey. I also feel that it was a part of my personal growth, and that it recalibrated that old moral compass of mine, one more time. It is painful but adjusted, yet again.

AN UNLIKELY CHOICE.....???

CHAPTER 25

Now, I have pictured and found myself in many arenas of medicine, but School Nursing was not one of them. I had a brief clinical experience during my ADN studies with home health care and it was not my "cup of tea." I did not like that, and the thought of sitting all day in an office in a school was not something I ever thought would be in my future. After a year off, I began doing some substitute teaching at neighboring districts. My daughter, now a teacher at a local high school, said their school always needed someone to fill in for teachers out for the day. It sounded like a nice, benign, non-committed type thing, something to break up the monotony of semi-retirement and soul searching, and keep my mind fresh and exercised. I processed myself in to the two neighboring districts and was called several times a month to come and "sub" for the day, as needed.

I covered classes from first grade, government, history, biology, chemistry, physics, and music. When asked to teach a Music class, my first question was, "Do I have to sing, or play an instrument"? When told no, I was there! It was a music class in an elementary school, and we showed a film about a wind harp. It was fascinating, however, I saw every grade that day, and I have to admit, it was nothing like my teaching adult education. There was lots of nose blowing, crying, shoe tying, toileting accidents, and testing the substitute lady....which I understand is the usual.

Later I was called in to be a guest teacher in a first grade room, and I suspect that every one of them cried at some point in the day, but not at the same time. Again, lots of tattling, shoe tying, nose wiping, wet pants, and crying. My skills as a teacher were sorely tested in the elementary school setting. I really do not think I am cut out for this job either.

Next month, I was called to be a guest at the high school, physics, if I recall correctly. The students were very smart, and very naughty. They were taking turns making trips to the bathroom, and the toileting pass was a toilet seat. I don't think we got much done that day, other than everyone went home with dry pants. I swore off high school that day, as I did not feel prepared to deal with their antics. Was I in for a surprise in my future!

As the school year drew to an end and we enjoyed summer, I decided that I was about ready to go back to work fulltime. I just did not know where, or doing what. I knew I did not want to do hospital Nursing again....too old and too tired. I just needed to find just the right place for me.

It is painfully obvious now, I suspect, that my attempts to re-invent myself were a struggle that I was seriously in need of, and not very successful with. I do need to find my niche....I have a $30,000.00 education, and need to put it to work at some level! My healing is about complete, and now I am ready to get up, brush myself off, and saddle up! There is something out there for me, I just know it!

As I went by one of the District Administrative offices that I was a guest teacher for to submit some paperwork, I was confronted by the Secretary for Human Resources. She said, "Hey, you are a RN, aren't you?" I replied that I was, and she proceeded to tell me that I should apply for the School Nurse position offered in the district that had just been posted. I laughed and said, "I don't think I want to work full-time....and I am getting old....and I don't know what School Nurses do...." Well, she said, she was going to put my information on the desk of the gentleman who was interviewing for the position, so I should go home and wait for a call. I went home, and within three hours, I was called by the Director of that service, and I had an interview set up for the next morning, just like that! Close a door, and open a window, right?

I went for the interview, with no resume support except that of women's healthcare. That few years, long ago, in the Pediatrician's office was there, but nothing recent. I guess the interview went well, as I was offered the job at the end of the meeting, and quoted a salary that was twice what I was making teaching in adult education! Wow!! Okay, I think this might be working out just fine. I can work full time, I suppose. I went home, my husband and I celebrated my good luck, and I was on my way!

Apparently, in this particular district, School Nursing is within the arena of Special Education. I had lots to learn, and the thought of being surrounded by children with disabilities was daunting to me. I was having visions of my last career choice, and wondering if I could do this! I recall, during the interview, too, that the Director stated that the job included a lot of paperwork and parent support, assessments and provision of resources to families, and just a lot of office work. Can I do this? Of course I can!

My first duty, to end the summer, was to attend a New School Nurse Orientation in one of our mountain towns. I spent three days there, in the hotel, with about one hundred other new...and old....School Nurses at different stages of career development. It was sometimes overwhelming, very busy, based on networking and collaboration, but fulfilling. It was interesting, scary, and I realized quickly that School Nursing was not what I thought it would be! It was more academic, with paperwork and lots of phone calling, with little to no ice packs, band-aids, and ace wraps. This was just what that knowledgeable Director had promised. I managed to hang on to most of the information I learned, and as I digested this new knowledge, I armed myself with it and when local school classes began, I was a new School Nurse!

SCHOOL NURSING... MY NEW PRE-RETIREMENT NURSING LIFE !!!

CHAPTER 26

For my first day of Orientation for the District, we met in a large meeting room with all the new teachers, therapists, etc., and I was on my way. The first day was a lot of general departmental housekeeping and necessary information for the new hires. The amazing thing about this job was that it is about one mile from my own home. No more of the grueling long drives up a freeway in inclement weather to fight my way into a building and to a job I had grown to hate. We were even put on school busses and driven around the district at the end of the week, with our sack lunches....how long had it been, right? We visited every school in the district, eleven at the time, I believe. I felt appreciated and special! Now, we were told to go to our assigned schools, and I had two, and meet our Administrators and staff. This was really getting interesting!

I cheerfully drove to my "home school", and first met the wonderful Assistant Principal. What a kind lady, and the exact person you would want to oversee your elementary child. She was most welcoming and friendly, a kind and supportive lady, about my own age. Until her retirement, I sought support, knowledge, guidance, and just warm love from this beautiful lady. She was a shining example for me. Anyway, she showed me around, introduced me to staff, and then took me in to meet the current Principal.

Now, this lady who was the Principal of this school was a tall, nice looking black woman, highly educated and obviously well respected. She stood, shook my hand, and immediately, seriously asked me, "What do you see being a School Nurse is?" Well now, I had not exactly thought of that....so I thought a minute, and said, "Well, I see myself responsible for everyone in the school.....now I know that I am responsible for the students, but I feel, as a Nurse, I must be on duty for everyone.....staff, visitors, students, and everyone here." Her face erupted into a huge grin, and she said, "Welcome to our school, and I just think we are going to enjoy having you as our Chief Medical Officer!" That was the first day of my first year there, and this lady and I instantly bonded. I felt amazing respect for both she and her Assistant Principal, and I knew instantly that we were going to make a good team! I felt the kinship between these two ladies, and was eager to partner with them.

Now, the other school I was assigned to was not quite as welcoming, but I did develop a good relationship with that staff too. I worked between schools, attempting to learn my duties and assume the responsibilities that came my way. I was to attend meetings for students who were struggling with education, and exhibiting some behaviors not becoming to either themselves or their learning environment. I quickly learned my way around the computer program, providing documentation that I was required to present, to support students with special needs. I occasionally saw a student in the health room for some complex or confounding issue beyond the expertise of the first aid staff.

Secretaries provide the first aid for students with bandages, temperature taking, tummy aches, and courtesy calls home for a variety of illnesses, injuries, and ailments that befall students in an elementary school. I was to be notified when the issue was larger than they were comfortable managing. I was to come and assess and determine what could be done for the student in need, occasionally making those phone calls home.

I soon learned that many students have complex behavioral and emotional issues, the result of society today, and families that are fragmented and struggling to survive. I worked with a wonderful Psychologist who was totally dedicated to these students, and I learned masses of information from her, working side-by-side with her for these children.

She and I laughed and cried over students and their situations, wiped their tears, cleaned dirt from under their nails (that was dirt, wasn't it?), washed soiled jackets on cold days, replaced wet tennis shoes and socks on snowy days, walked students to class with loving support, and served in too many ways to recall. You see, this is a population of children who were experiencing high needs, due to a war on another continent. Also, these students have parents in the military, and the war has taken their parents (often both) away, and we are left to try and hold the small, fragile families together. I love the challenge and know I have a lot of love and support to give. They have my Nursing heart! I just might be in the right place, now in the sunset of my career....I can do this for a few years until retirement.

One day, as I was working in my office down the hall, I was summoned by my Principal, and asked to go to a certain classroom to pick up a child. The teacher had buzzed the office, asking for support in the classroom, and everyone else was busy. When I arrived, there stood a child, naked as the day she was born, and the whole class had their heads down on their desks, with their eyes closed, and singing quietly. The teacher stated that the child had a "melt-down", and had stripped off her clothes and had run around the room, screaming. This insightful and experienced teacher had immediately seen where this was going, and had quickly said, "Boys & Girls! Please quickly put your heads down on your desk, close your eyes, and stay there, singing the birthday song, until I tell you to sit up!"

They did as told, and we quickly grabbed a coat and removed the child from under the desk and whisked her off to the office in a large baggy coat. We retrieved her clothes, and the class went back to their studies. This occurred several times throughout the year, as the child had learned that stripping naked was a good way to get out of class. Discipline became the job of the Psychologist and other staff, and I was able to return to my typical "Nursing" duties.

Another day in the school, I was asked to come to the office to see a child with an injury. Now, you have to understand that when I am called, the injury is likely serious or complex. When I got there, a child sat there with big eyes, crying, and said he had a rock up his nose. Now, we have a playground outside with the perfect sized rocks on it to shove up noses and into ears....so I had him block the opposite nostril, take a deep breath, and blow as hard as he could, which he did. Immediately, the rock flew across the room, and he burst out laughing & crying at the same time! Good job, I said......and he went back to class. Problem solved! Crisis averted! They don't teach these things in Nursing school, but having a grown up son helps....as he and I have experienced most of the events I am called to the office for....rashes, rocks, falls, and everything little kids think of as they grow and experiment with life. We all know that the world is just one big science experiment to young children.....right?

On another occasion I was called up for a child who had gone all over the sidewalk and picked up the nice blue "candy" sprinkled around on a snowy day, and attempted to eat it. She immediately spit it out, as it tasted "nasty", according to her teacher. She thought it was "candy pop rocks" that pop in your mouth....but it was sidewalk ice melt! I quickly consulted with the custodian, he checked his bag labels and it was non-toxic! I called poison control and they verified with us it was not injurious, and we were relieved. I guess a little blue candy scattered on a sidewalk is considered a gift to a Kindergartner, right? Shame on those companies for making such tasty looking ice melt!

Another day, I saw a child who had spilled hot chicken noodle soup down the front of him at lunch, while walking to his seat. I saw him, applied a cooling cloth with ice water, he was soothed, and he returned to class. Within an hour, I was called to see another child for the same thing....something was NOT right here! I treated the second child, and went to talk to the kitchen manager. She said she had to serve the soup at a certain temperature, based on regulations, and after a long conversation, I saw that she was not able to eliminate the very hot soup from the menu. I went to talk to the wise Principal about this dilemma, and she quietly picked up the phone and called the kitchen supervisor off site. She stated to him, "My Chief Medical

Officer has deemed that these children cannot carry hot bowls of soup, at your required temperature, from the line to their seats without burning themselves, so we have ourselves a real problem. What are you going to do about this?" He immediately arranged to have the soup ladled at their seats, and these small children were relieved of this treacherous journey with a tray and bowl of hot liquids.

This wonderful Principal passed away about a year ago, and as I attended her memorial service, I was reminded of her dedication to these children. She was a shining beacon in my learning to become a school Nurse. She often told us, "Always put that child first, and you won't go wrong!".....and she was right. They are valuable and precious resources for our world yet to come. We must handle them with care!

On my birthday, and to this day, I anticipate the arrival of a chorale of students, at all grade levels, in my office, with a birthday song! This is the delight of my birthday every year.....no gifts of anything, but the beautiful voices of children singing loudly and enthusiastically! Joy! I hear birthday songs everyday of the year, and the voices of children fill the hallways of the school every day. I also love when the Kindergarten next door is practicing songs..... birthday, Christmas, Valentines, Graduation.....their voices are pure delight! To have them sing to me is Heaven!

During the summer I do not hear those voices, and when I return in the Fall for the new school year, I relish in the sounds of children laughing, talking, giggling, and chattering among themselves. I cherish their stopping by and talking about everything in their worlds. They are our future! It is pure Joy!

Speaking of the Kindergarten classroom next door, it is pure delight when they are enjoying Kindergarten Graduation. They gather in the gym in their tiny white mortar board hats, sing proudly of their achievements, and everyone gathers in the cafeteria for punch and cake. Now, everyone in the building is recruited to cut and serve these massive cakes and pour gallons of punch for the proud families. I enjoy participating, and one year we had an especially large class of graduates. We moved the reception outside on a beautiful day, and as my colleagues and I cut and served the cake, the butter cream icing melted, as it was a warm day, and we had quite the mess on our hands! Everyone had a wonderful time and that is what counted!

One day a little boy arrived late to school, and when the secretaries asked him where he had been and why he was late, he had this answer. He said he had to put a leash on his snake and it took a while to get the snake to walk to school beside him. He then proceeded to tell them that the snake was tied to the utility pole outside the school by the road. What an imagination and story! It did not work, understandably, and he was sent off to class with a tardy slip. Dawdling, would be my guess, right?

On any given day, I arrive at the elementary school and am greeted with a virtual mix of almost anything you could think of in attire! Often my other school is not on the same calendar plan for dress up. On one day, I arrived and everyone's hair was done up in all sorts of "do's"....colors, wigs, braids, frizzes, and about anything you could think of. Apparently, it was "Crazy Hair Day"....a reward for having completed certain state testing. Another day, I arrived to be greeted by EVERYONE on staff, including administration, in pajamas and robes....another reward for having read a special number of books over a certain period of time. Much more common, is to arrive to a staff and students in sports jerseys, representing their favorite NFL team, jeans on the last Friday of the month, and everyone wearing ties, clothing backwards, pink for Breast Cancer Day, or one single color, such as red or black to represent Drug Free Zone. Apparently, to dress inappropriately for school, with permission, is a great incentive to perform and enjoy doing it! Middle school is typically not allowed to wear athletic gear, so to be dressed in sport clothing is a treat. They also are occasionally seen wearing crazy socks, 50's clothing, and, oh yes, Nerd Day is a big one! Nursing in schools is a whole different experience. It is something I am so glad I am a part of!

Another day, all the Kindergartners were out at recess. Now, they quickly learn that any need that takes them back into the building will take up all their recess time. A little girl went to the teacher, and showed her a scratch that had occurred on some of the playground equipment outside, and she said, "I don't need to go inside and get a band-aid, because the blood came out, and then it just went back inside.....so I am fine!" Creativity and necessity.....that is how they roll!

Did I mention that I also check scalps and hair for lice? Well, I do that fairly regularly. One particularly rough week with frequent lice checks, a child came up and I searched her hair, and found both lice and nits. I contacted parents, and they picked her up, taking my suggestions for cleaning the house and bedding. I also gave them instructions to shampoo her hair with special shampoo, and permission for her to return to school the next day, after treatment.

The following day, I noticed a child sitting in the office on the bench, she had on a hoodie, and appeared withdrawn and sad. When I asked her to take her hoodie off in the building, as per rules, she did, and it was this little girl! Her Father had shaved her head to rid her of the lice, as he had experienced when he was a child. He said that was the only true way to get rid of them! I was shocked and disappointed for this child, as she had to spend the next several months trying to get her hair grown out to even an acceptable length! If I have not learned anything else in this Nursing assignment, it is that we DO NOT GET TO PICK OUR FAMILIES! Makes us wonder, right?

One of the most interesting aspects of School Nursing is that of the variety of students we have. We have wee small people that have bright minds, trapped in disabled bodies, healthy children who are sorely neglected as to hygiene and self-care, tidy and bright students who take pride in both education and good healthy habits, and bright students who are neglected pitifully. We see no color, race, intellect, behaviors, or abilities....but only children coming to school, either willingly, or not. We love them all!

Our students are members of the military community, as I mentioned, and in the beginning of the Iraq war we lost some soldiers who were parents of our students. It is a sad observation and task to see an Administrator sitting quietly and explaining to a young group of students that someone has lost their parent in combat. Everyone in the building participates in the support and love for that family. We experienced that too many times, and it was one of the toughest parts of School Nursing for me. No child should have to deal with that aspect of life…..the loss of a parent. They are brave, forgiving, and stronger than many adults, and they are thankfully resilient.

That part has quieted now, and we stand daily and pledge our allegiance to a flag that flies over a country that is free because of the parents of these brave children. We Nurses of these children provide more than bandages and ice. We provide love, support, and understanding for these families that have given so much to our country…..some have given parents and we cannot forget that. My pledge to those families is that I will do my best to take care of their children while they fight a war on the other side of the globe.

A DAY....OR WEEK...IN THE LIFE OF A SCHOOL NURSE

The first day of school is always interesting and challenging! Everyone shows up dressed up in brand new clean clothes, shoes, socks, carrying a brand new backpack loaded with supplies for the year, with their names carefully written on everything. Large piles of boxes of tissues, glue, crayons, hand sanitizer (something I never had to take to school, for sure!), lined paper, and pencils. Everything and everyone is shiny and new, everyone smells great, we all give hugs and greetings for another upcoming successful school year. New teachers nervously greet new families and students are made welcome, being seated in classrooms throughout the building. Everyone is excited, routines are being set, rules are discussed, lunch is chaotic but everyone is fed, and everyone is ready to start the new school year.

Now, in the Kindergarten rooms, there is lots of crying, reluctance, fear of the unknown, and separation anxiety....and that is just the parents! Most of the kiddos are anxious to come to school! They are ready and shiny and new. A new year has begun!

After a few weeks, routines are in place, cubbies are filled with supplies, and everyone knows everyone.....or at least everyone in the classroom, and parents have actually learned how to survive at home throughout the day.....well, most of them have....without their younglings. Life has assumed some measure of normal in school.

We enjoy, once a year, dressing up like a Storybook Character on

Storybook Day! Now this is fun! I have a big tub of costumes in my basement to this day containing costumes for Pippi Longstocking, Dr. Seuss, Scarecrow from Wizard of Oz, and many wigs to make characters. On one particular day, I was dressed as Pippi Longstocking, and our LPN was dressed as the Scarecrow. About noon, someone called us to the playground to check a child who had fallen from the monkey bars, and was possibly injured. We rushed out to care for her, and as she had a history of back injuries, we had her lie still while the office called in an ambulance to transport her to have her checked out in the ER.

Upon the arrival of the EMS team, our Kindergarten teacher opened the playground gate for the 911 team....and she was dressed perfectly as Cinderella, right up to the tiara! Under the monkey bars were Pippi and Scarecrow....and the EMS team just nodded, smiled, rolled their eyes, and went about their business of caring for the child. Later they said they thought it weird, but, hey, EMS sees a lot of weird stuff, right?

Any fairly common day rolls by, and we find soiled underwear in the restrooms, plugged up sinks and toilets with paper towels & toilet paper, and children locked in stalls without a clue as to how to unlock. I have escorted hysterical and screaming students to the front office, run alongside students on the run, attempting to stop them from exiting the building, and removed all manner of items, such as paperclips, rocks, beans, pieces of plastic, and paper wads from noses and ears. I have stood in the parking lot between an older student and the road, with him threatening to run into danger, and sat with crying students when they are being questioned or evaluated by DHS.

Other children have "melt-downs" and sit in my office on the couch kicking and screaming, crying, howling, and making any and all kinds of noises, as they try and pull themselves together. Soon, they do just that, and return to class to finish the day. Now, tell me, have you not ever had that kind of day? I have! Sometimes we just need a place where we can get it out and then move on.....right? Nurses seem to be seen by overwrought students as a safe place to be

themselves, and parents have that same feeling....Nurses are safe....
and I love that!

Seizures become a commonplace event, having found students
on a floor, unresponsive, leaving me to determine just who they are
and what happened to them. Sometimes we are witness to the event,
and other times not. Middle school students have a propensity to be
dramatic and what we term "drama queens". It appears to take three
or four young ladies to accompany a crying female student to the
health room for any type medical attention, with much to do around
them. Male students seem to be able to "soldier up" to the need, and
arrive often limping and hopping, with no fan fair, however, the
ladies need much more emotional support and attention by friends
in order to get prompt and efficient help.

Sorting out the reality versus the diversion from class is always
tricky, and much thought goes into the process. First of all we
assess the physical symptoms, add that to the data gathered, such
as temperature, blood pressure, and pulse oxygen. Then we have
a conversation with the student, which includes typical medical
assessment questions, but also we add such inquiries as "What class
are you in, and what are you doing right now in class?" Sometimes
we find them avoiding a class, occasionally it is social avoidance,
and sometimes they are actually ill, but do not appear so! It is sort
of like being a detective, as we sort out everything, and soon get
to the reality. I am supported by awesome secretaries who know
the students very well, and quickly contribute information, and
absolutely know the "frequent flyers" who are ditching class.....and
the kiddos that seldom seek attention in the office, therefore making
this process so much easier and accurate.

December and the upcoming Holiday/Winter Break in the
elementary school is particularly exhilarating! Children seem to
become more active and enthusiastic as the holiday season nears!
School is particularly tough on them at this time, and we feel the
full brunt of it.....so, we just go with it! Every December, we are
freed about midway through the month for Winter Break. On that
last day we all are excited, as the different classes have their little

holiday parties, complete with candy, cookies, and some healthy treats, singing, dancing, hugs, laughter, and joy over the upcoming exit from classes for at least two weeks. I think it is, however a race to the parking lot between staff and students, as we staff anticipate this exodus equally!!

One elementary school with a super energetic Principal chooses to line up all the teachers, dress them funny, but appropriately, for the Holiday Assembly. They sing and dance around the gym to the tune of the 12 Days of Christmas, and the kids are very entertained! The funniest sight is that of all the men on staff, coaches, administrators, and those who work in the building, dressed as elves in tu-tu's, holding hoops, with ribbons flying, singing and dancing around the gym at the assembly. I think they were the dancing lords 'a leaping... and the other teachers include the maids 'a milking, geese 'a laying, and so forth. What laughter from the students this draws!

Everyone is walking around the building all day wearing a Santa hat or elf hat, food is piled up in the lounge, and everyone snacks and eats, therefore gaining several pounds over this holiday event! At the final assembly just before dismissal, a local big box store donates a girls and a boys bicycle to the school. As we are always encouraging perfect attendance, all children in the building that have managed perfect attendance for the Fall semester are eligible for a win. Their names are put into a bag, and one lucky boy and one lucky girl is drawn out of the bag as the winner of a bicycle. This is always a great event, as every child with perfect attendance has a chance to win! The smiles are huge for the winners! The children all sing holiday carols during this assembly, and it is a wonderful exit to the Winter Break! Nothing sends us off like a big gym full of children joyfully laughing and singing holiday songs!

Most of the school year is day to day activities that are typical. State testing is very stressful for the students, teachers, and staff alike. The hallways are cordoned off and silence is the word for the weeks that define these required tests. At the Middle school, some assigned staff member walks past with a typical grocery shopping cart full of cell phones. Each phone has a sticky note labeling its owner, confiscated during testing, to be returned at the end of the day. As a Nurse, I sit quietly in my office, working on my upcoming year's tasks, assembling forms for the first few weeks of school, and just being quiet. Our Health room almost has the chirp of crickets it is so quiet, as no one is allowed to wander in and out, and up and down the halls. The building is quiet and still.

When testing is done for the students, pizza parties abound and joy is spread over the whole kingdom! Everything is amazingly back to normal! Joyful noise returns!

Unfortunately, like all communities, we have wonderful days, and the occasional tragedy. After all, a school is a small community of people. One school year, we suffered the loss of a young Kindergartner. He was not a very healthy child, to begin with, and as the year wore on, he continued on the path of this chronic illness. He finally succumbed to it at home on a day he was not in attendance at school. This family was impoverished, experiencing a run of very bad luck, with disability and illness in the family. There were several other siblings in the very tiny home. Our school had previously adopted this family for Christmas, providing food, clothing, toys, and everything we could to see that they had a nice holiday.

I had seen this little guy in my health room the day before, for some health issues, called home, and they were doing the best they could to take care of him, but in my heart, have to assume that it was just his time to be called home. I suspect one never is prepared to lose a child, but sadly, it happens. When it does, I really do see a genuine outpouring of love and caring. We organized meals to be taken to the home every day for several weeks, until visiting relatives finally had to leave to return to their lives in other states. Our local big box store donated clothing for the child's funeral, and additionally provided garments for every family member of this family to attend his funeral appropriately dressed. A local funeral chapel donated their services, and many staff members, myself included, attended the visitation and/or funeral. It was a sad and somber time, as we laid this beautiful child to rest, but one does what is necessary to care for the family.

It is both gratifying and reassuring to see how people pull

together when in crisis, and where, but a school, would one see this strength when any family is at its lowest, emotionally. They somehow managed to get through this, and have since moved away, but I still cherish his smile and memory, knowing he is in a wonderful place, where children go to run and play, healthy and happy.

On a happier note, we all do enjoy field trips, right? I find them one of my "perks" to go on a field trip with my students. I have to admit, the younger the student, the more fun the trip......let's face it....admit it.....middle school students are just not quite as much fun, right?

Okay, I stand corrected.....I guess it is in the eye of the beholder! Let's see....blowing noses, tying shoes, pushing a stroller or wheelchair through dirt trails, zipping jackets, picking stickers out of all body parts, & spilling juice all over.....versus....foul smells & sounds at the back of the bus, girl drama, crying off and on, moving seat to seat on the bus, sneaking substances, walking all over the bus, & keeping up with site wanderers....hummmm....maybe about the same overall! Anyway, I do love to go on the field trips, for all ages, most days. I have stumbled through pumpkin patches, helped carry a pumpkin the size of the child, picked stickers out of hands, attempted to teach a young child how to use a port-a-potty, sat in the dirt having a picnic lunch, ridden on the back of a wooden wagon while singing songs, sat in theaters trying to keep little people quiet, toileted every single child on the bus at some given time, and reminded the older kiddos that just because the bus has a restroom, everyone does NOT have to go back there and use it , and then come out making all manner of sounds and disgusting comments at the condition of the toilet.

I do enjoy the field trips, and the School Nurse does go when a medically challenged student is included and a parent cannot attend, and they are <u>ALWAYS</u> included. I love the feeling of being there for them while they enjoy what all other students enjoy, and feel a part of things, as they should. Nursing is disguised in many costumes, and creating an environment of happiness and inclusion is one of those.....for our youngest and all patients. School Nursing provides us that opportunity and good fortune.

One of our favorite activities in an elementary school is that of Professional Dress Day. The students are encouraged to dress "professionally" for class one day per week, as designated, and to show that they know how to dress up like a professional. Now some of the dress up attire is interesting....princess dresses, tu-tus', and my all time favorite, formal dance attire. I guess it takes time and training to become an appropriately dressed professional. The boys look so handsome in their shirt and ties, hair slicked back, and a bit like they look on picture day!

In this particular school, the Counselor is a trainer for service dogs for the disabled. Now this particular Counselor is also the leader of the dress up days, so as everyone in the school is dressed up, why would we not expect the dog in training to follow suit? McDogg is always seen dressed appropriately the with attire of a white shirt collar and a tie. He looks very professional, I must say! This dog is a part of everything in the building, and joins into all the fun! He is a fine example of good behavior, good looks, and professionalism.

Just by his presence, he leads the children, calms, supports, listens attentively, and trains children in the basic rule that they are NOT to pet a dog in a green jacket, as he is officially on duty, and when his jacket is off, they are to ask for petting privileges. This teaches children to ask first, pet after permission, and to NEVER pet a working dog on duty. What a gift to a young population to learn from, and a wonderful loving support by one of our four-legged friends in training. Through the years, we have seen many dogs come and go from this wonderful trainer, and are proud to know they are out there assisting someone with physical or emotional disabilities, as needed. These dogs sit with crying students, are read to at length, and are hugged when the child is least huggable. I still have my favorite, and he has moved on to his assigned family some time ago. I just wonder if he still wears his white collar & tie on special days?

Recently, I had a child come up to me in the hallway for a hug, and said to me, in all sincerity, "Are you that cookin' lady on TV?" I know who she means, and I say to her, "No, sweetie, but I do love to cook....and hope to be as good a cook as her, and be on

TV someday!" My Counselor was standing in the hallway nearby, chuckling, and now he takes great joy in calling me by this well known TV personality's name when he sees me ....I guess it is my southern accent and greying hair.....oh, and my loud, happy laugh with the kids around me. She is a beautiful and cheerful, bigger than life lady. I find it one of my highest compliments ever!

One of my jobs is to care for staff, as well as children. I have assessed many rashes, lumps, bumps, and feelings of illnesses with my staff. We have seen many babies born, broken legs, and a myriad of illnesses come and go. On any given day, there are always at least two or three pregnancies going on in a single building, every year. I have assessed swelling legs, blood pressures, and sent some off to their MD for immediate care.

In one of my buildings I had a teacher, who was pregnant with her third (and later, fourth) child, and had a history of very fast labors. Now, being an OB Nurse by experience, I was the watchful one. I had cautioned this teacher to have a towel on standby in her room, just in case. I had also made certain that she had left phone numbers with the front office staff to call her husband, just in case. We were absolutely ready! One day, I was called by the office to go to her classroom and check on her, as she had buzzed in on her intercom, asking for me. I grabbed my stethoscope (old OB Nurses never forget!) and headed for her room. When I arrived, she had sent her class out next door, and was standing there in a puddle of amniotic fluid. I quickly got her sat down, checked her baby's heartbeat, verified it was fine, and called the office to call her husband to meet her at the hospital. One of our staff was available to drive her, and she was soon on her way to deliver this anxious baby! She did make it to the hospital in time, and soon we had pictures of a beautiful little boy! I just did not want to deliver this child in our school. I could, but would choose not to, by all means!

One day, as we celebrated Costume Day on October 31st, I dressed as Raggedy Ann. Mid-morning, I was called to an elementary school for a teacher who was having a minor health issue and as I arrived, I was greeted by the Principal, who was very concerned about his young teacher. I assessed her, and it was my recommendation that she notify her personal physician, and arrange to be seen by him right away, however it was not a transportable emergency. As the Principal came into the Health Room, I was leaning over the teacher, taking her blood pressure and assessing her pulse oxygen levels, and I noticed him stifling a laugh. He said, "I am sorry, but to have my staff treated by a rag doll is just such a chuckle for me." We did know that she would be fine, and she was taken by her husband to be seen and returned to class that afternoon. Raggedy Ann then went on about her usual business about the school. WOW! I do love this job!

Overall, working in schools is energizing and fulfilling. It has its good days and bad days, but working with children, of all ages, is always exhilarating. As I have had a Middle School (sixth through eighth grades) added to my duty, it has become an exercise in understanding all ages. I still love to get up in the morning and come to work. I still anticipate the upcoming year in August, as we come back onto campus. I still cannot wait to meet the Kindergarteners in the class next to my office every year, in the Elementary School. Kids are always gregarious and challenging, but provide me, an old lady now, with love and laughs. Hardly a day goes by that I do not get a good laugh, an opportunity to be supportive and loving to someone, and to dry tears or share a funny story. This just might be my dream job!

As I reach the sunset of my Nursing career, I am in the best possible place I could be! I am so blessed to have this opportunity of surrounding myself with children of all ages. I find myself denying imminent retirement, as I wonder often what I would be giving up. I would miss the children, loving opportunities to be the change in a child's life, and making a difference......thoughts to ponder......

UNIMAGINABLE TRAGEDY IN A SCHOOL.....YET AGAIN

We are on Winter Break for two weeks. As I put these thoughts down, there has occurred a horrific tragedy. A mentally ill young man has entered an Elementary School, far from our town, shooting and killing twenty, six and seven year old children, and six staff members, plus his own Mother in their home. Now, I cannot watch this happen without it touching my soul on a very deep, personal level. Working in an Elementary and Middle School every day, I have to accept that in today's society, we are at risk for these things happening. I realize that no matter what preventatives we put in place as a school district, they can all be overridden and security to our buildings breached. Schools cannot become fortresses, with a prison-like feel of doors locked, armed guards at the doors. They are, after all, schools.

I do not understand my feelings within, other than the fact that I have grown up and lived all my life with a feeling of safety and refuge in schools. When hurricanes struck my coastal hometown when I was a child, we sought refuge in schools because they were harbors of safety. Gatherings were held in schools, and just like churches, they were considered beacons of safety. They were the place to go for enrichment and love, a hallmark of goodness in the community. Now, during the past several years there have been horrible shootings in schools, senseless killing of children who certainly have no investment in the evil this represents. Why anyone would choose to commit mass shootings of our innocents can only be explained away through mental illness, and enormous evil in a soul that is troubled and out of control.

I cannot imagine what it would be like to find myself in that horrible situation. Everyday that I am at my Elementary School, I am approached by at least one, but more often, dozens of children of all ages, for hugs, during their busy days. It is not uncommon, as they return in their organized lines coming from art, computer class, PE, lunch and recess, for one child to run to me for a hug, and before I know it, every single child in the class walks past me and reaches for a hug. I often find myself apologizing to the teachers for the delay in their return to class this causes, however, they just smile and assure me that it is just fine....everyone needs a hug and they understand that! As long as there is a child reaching for one of my hugs, I will be passing them out! Who could turn them away with any conscience? One has to wonder just how many hugs they get away from school....

As I watch the television coverage of the small, young lives lost in this display of evil, I wonder when they had their last hug. I also push away the thoughts that if, in my rush to go to another task, I should deny one of my sweet students, and an event like this occurred in our building, how I would regret it. We have no idea how long we have, and in the blink of an eye, we can be gone, they can be gone, so I take away from this event the plan to love my little guys well, at every opportunity, for they deserve it.

I also wonder how hard it must have been for families all over our nation to send their youngsters off to school this morning, innocent and vulnerable to the evils in this world, and the potential of not ever seeing them again. I called my grown son and asked him his feelings when he sent our precious six year old grandson off this morning, and he agreed it was hard. He has even taken steps of contacting the school district about reviewing their safety standards. That is reassuring to me, as I must have instilled into him something strong and loving, to try and make his child's world safer. He is a great Daddy, so I feel assured that there is still goodness and light in a world gone astray in so many ways.

My grown daughter now is a High School teacher, and I ponder her safety also, as she goes about her day with her students. High School can be a treacherous and volatile site, with emotions running high between students and staff. She is a bold and brave woman, fearless and confident, and I know, without a doubt what she would do. She would jump directly into the melee, fighting for her students and herself without fear. That is a Mother's concern, for sure. As for our children's safety, I guess we just have to have faith and hold them in our hearts every moment in time.

I wondered too, if, as a staff member in that building, I would have been brave enough to run toward the gunman, and not hover under my desk to prevent risk to my own life. I conferred with my husband, a Viet Nam veteran, who spent many years in combat and firefights. I asked him how you would know what to do, or what anyone would choose to do. His reply was, "You won't know until faced with that decision....I have seen brave, bold men run like scared rabbits, and frail, fearful men fight to the death, so you just don't know." I guess one could not know whether, in that moment of panic, which way you would run.

I like to think I would seek to save the children in my near vicinity, and make it safe for them, risking my own life. Maybe I would make that valiant attempt to take the "bad guy" out, thereby saving the children.....maybe I would run and lock myself away in a closet, or tremble under my own desk in my office, listening to the merciless shooting of innocent victims under my watch. God willing, I will never have to make that choice, but one never knows.

I pray for these small souls called home too soon, and the families that stand at the edge of sanity, while giving them up. I know there is a bigger and better plan, and this is one of those times that we are not to understand, we are to just rely on our faith and God's plan to accept what we cannot change. .... "Suffer the little children to come unto me....." is little comfort to those families, but we all know they are at peace now, and no longer feel fear. There surely is a huge hole where all their lives were in that community and within those families. I cannot even imagine it!

God bless the children and the brave staff that sacrificed their own lives for others.

......YOU CANNOT MAKE THIS STUFF UP......

CHAPTER 29

Children are our validation that life goes on....and we can smile, laugh, and love! I cannot imagine my life without the small smiles, lost teeth, giggles, sitting and singing on the toilet across from my office, and the little people that I am surrounded by at work. I have the best job in the world, and am not sure when I can retire! I just love what I do!

So, I was recently in my office and was called down to see a little boy who had been struck on the arm with a flying soccer ball. I assessed his injury, and he assured me that he was actually the strongest kicker in the class. He proceeded to tell the story of the whole game, blow by blow. Typically, we get the whole instant replay....anyway, I checked him out thoroughly, he was good, so I provided him with an ice pack, and sent him happily back to class with his battle wound. He was the game hero!

Now this whole time, sitting on a cot nearby, with a giant filled backpack and her coat on, was a tiny, precious little dark-eyed Kindergarten girl. She was observing all I was doing, quietly. I hardly even realized she was there, as her needs appeared to have been met by the office staff. She was waiting for her parent to pick her up.

As I was assessing the young man, a second little Kindergarten girl came into the health room and sat on a chair. The Secretary had taken care of her, having questioned her quietly and left to call her parent. I turned, and as I was leaving the room, this very loud but sweet little girl voice, boomingly said, "Excuse me....Mewwy and me are sick!" I turned and asked her if someone had checked on her and she said, again boomingly, ..."Oh yes, I am going home.... but Mewwy is sick too." I asked "mewwy" if she had been taken care of, and she nodded that she had.. The first little girl said, again, boomingly.... "I thweww up in the twash can and have to go home, and my Mommy is coming, but Mewwy has diwwea...." I looked at "Mewwy", and she said, "It was gweeen, and a wot....so I am going home too." No filters....that is what it is.....these children have NO filters yet....and it is a beautiful, beautiful thing. There is still time to teach them the rules of life, but right now, I just LOVE these little unfiltered guys.......!

Another day, I sat in my office next door to the Kindergarten class.....and I still say I have the best seat in the house. I listened to the teaching going on next door. Now, I am old, and these beautiful, impressionable, innocent children have to learn everything that we already know in life. They are pure, innocent, impressionable little souls, and it is our duty to help them develop into winners in life. This is something we seldom think of, but take for granted. As the Dr. Martin Luther King, Jr. Holiday approaches, we enjoy a Monday off from work in respect of his hard work with desegregation and the racial issues of our past, as a nation. Now, these children do not have any idea about the ugly discriminations that blighted our country. Again, we forget that they are pure, blank slates, and un-imprinted souls.....with no knowledge of past events. We continue to forget this, so many times.

As I sat in my office, I listened, as the kind and patient Kindergarten teacher tried to explain, first of all, about the history of skin colors being big public decision makers. Those of who could eat in a restaurant, use a public restroom, attend a movie in a particular seat, and ride a bus, sitting anywhere they chose. These children are so young and innocent, it is really hard for them to perceive that behavior, and this teacher did such a marvelous of explaining it.

These impressionable little students were aghast that someone could not come with them to the local favorite hamburger place if their skin was not "pink". As I sat and listened to these innocent questions, and to her sincere and sensitive, but informational answers, I realized just why we celebrate Dr. King....and he must be up there smiling down on that classroom. We have achieved much of what he was leading us toward....as the children are finally becoming "colorblind" to these old ways, and instead, see no color or race in the classroom. They instead, embrace everyone as a person and see all as one. I had to smile, as it had never dawned on me either, as an educated woman, mother, and grandmother....just when does racism develop? Where does it come from? It certainly does NOT begin in our Kindergarten classrooms in the schools where I spend my days. If we could start with just the conversation that I heard in that classroom, our world would be a more tolerant, accepting, unbiased, and loving place.

Now, living in an office outside a Kindergarten is an interesting place. The restrooms are just across from my office, and sitting at my desk, well, I see it all. It is not uncommon to have a small person dance a jig into my office, jumping and hopping around, holding themselves, and needing assistance with a stubborn zipper or belt. I help with that, and then they rush off to the restroom, often failing to close a door, and the sounds are varied! Some sing, others just issue giant sighs of relief, and others simply talk to themselves or just talk out loud. They then rush back into my office and get the help they need to rearrange their clothing, closing zippers and belts, and turn and dash off. This frequently happens during recess, and these restrooms are the nearest to the outside playground. One can only imagine the hurry they are in, as their precious recess time is not to be taken up with toileting needs!

Each year this class holds "High Tea". The children are taught about the British history of taking tea in the afternoon, and it is a formal occasion. The children come to school in their "Sunday Best", all dressed up and curled and combed. They go to the cafeteria in pairs, two by two, holding hands, boy and girl, and sit and have cucumber sandwiches, and are served tea. For some, this is a wonderful event, while others are not so impressed....dressing up, sandwiches made with cucumbers....not their cup of tea! They are, however, very excited about the specialness of the day.....and the wonderful learning experience of another country.

They also learn a bit about France. I visited France several years ago and brought back a one-foot tall metal replica of the Eiffel Tower, in support of learning the history of several foreign countries. Now, you have to understand, these are the children of our military, and before they leave home as adults, they will likely have seen Germany, Japan, England, and several other foreign countries. This is simply a part of their lives on the move. We can only hope that we have contributed some curiosity and enthusiasm for their future journeys. They are the fortunate ones, as they are able to travel to foreign lands and learn a variety of things many children only read about.

I always provide positive support and eagerness for their upcoming "PCS", or military move, and talk to them about the beaches of the Carolinas & Georgia, the winter and holidays in Germany, the amazing culture in Japan, trying to create some enthusiasm for where they are headed. I also always remind them of the gift they are getting, just in travelling to foreign countries with both parents instead of standing on a tarmac or in a gym waving goodbye to their soldier parent(s). They are going as a family unit, and there is so much to see and do!

One day a child came to the Health Room with a zip baggie holding a yellow, waxy looking glob and several cotton tipped applicators. Now, the District policy is that we do not administer or apply anything to or into our students without a full MD order and a signed parental permission form. This is to provide the ultimate safety for the child, and provide legal coverage to ourselves. It is a common practice throughout all local school districts.

This little girl very maturely said, "This is for my cut inside my mouth....you see, I had some food cut my mouth, and it is sore. My Mom said if I put some of this 'hurricane' on my cut, it will numb it, and if I swallow it, it will just wear off and not hurt me." Okay, what I think we have here is some form of oral numbing medication like Xylocaine, not hurricane, and I am not willing to administer it without the appropriate orders and paperwork. Instead, I had this precious little girl rinse her mouth in cool water, or give her Mom a call to come and administer it....as that is her other option. She left the Health Room with a rinsed mouth, message left for Mom, and returned to class. Hurricane...Xylocaine....still do not administer.... you understand, right? In Nursing, rules are rules.....and we all must follow them.

THERE IS SOMETHING REALLY SPECIAL ABOUT MIDDLE SCHOOLERS!!

CHAPTER 30

Recently I was honored with a Nursing privilege that I have never experienced! One of our substitute secretaries at one of our schools has a wonderful son, a big handsome boy who is applying to West Point Academy. Just the application process is daunting and enormous, and his final step today, before submitting this important, life-altering packet, is to provide a documented current weight and height, signed by a Registered Nurse, preferably a School Nurse. I was kindly asked to do this for him. He was a graduate of our district and was stellar as a student. I was proud and flattered to do so, and he arrived, right on time, at his appointed time set by his parent with me. The "yes Ma'm", "no Ma'm" he answered with were phenomenal, and that kind of respect and dignified presence is seldom found in students today. He certainly exhibited himself as a cadet, and I will do my part to support him gain that opportunity. He loomed well above my five-foot stature, standing in his sock feet on my medical scale, and I had to call on our School Resource Officer to be able to reach the top of his head in order to measure his height. Again, I am both flattered and excited for him, and this is something I can do for him toward a life's journey that can mean success and a proud future. He spoke with a strong, confident voice, was polite, business-like, and focused. He made me proud to be able to support him, and I wish him the best. We have now gotten the news, several weeks after this, that he has received his appointment to West Point! Congratulations, you fine young man! Godspeed!

I just got an email from one of my schools' fifth grade teachers. She is having some concern with odorous bodies in her classroom. Now, normally this does not show itself until the weather warms up, and being February, with snow on the ground, it is surprising that it has appeared so early. Not to worry, I will take my video about good hygiene, self-respect, and dignity to the classroom on an upcoming Friday afternoon, and have that dialog with the whole fifth grade. They are blossoming adults, surging with hormones, and not always conscious about their personal upkeep. They have much more on their minds, and this is one of my duties....that of teaching them to take good care of their bodies on a daily basis.

I teach many classes, as time permits, about hand washing, hygiene, manners, and a variety of health based concerns. We talk about stinky tennis shoes worn with no socks, armpits, scrubbing faces until they gleam, not always choosing their favorite but cleanest dirty shirt.....and just odors in general. We also discuss nose picking, covering our mouth when we cough or sneeze, and sitting with our legs in an appropriate position, especially if they are young ladies! I don't recall these conversations ever being a part of my days at school, but came from home. My Mother, rest her soul, often reminded me that I always must go out with my best manners on, sit like a lady, and always take a bath and shampoo my hair at night. I can recall the old "spit and set" for my curls, eyebrows, or something like crumbs on my face. I also never recall seeing television commercials....and we did not have a television until I was twelve years old....that discussed hygiene products. This information came from our parents....and often! I feel that the kids today have a greater challenge in their worlds than we did as youngsters and adolescents, however, it is NOT rocket science....it is hygiene, for crying out loud! Wash, brush, wipe, and sniff every now and then......your friends will appreciate it!

They also have wonderful hearing due to the fact that the car radio or tape deck played only loud enough for those in the vehicle to hear the music. Everyday, families pull up to the curb, let a child out, and the music can be heard across the parking lot. I just look, and think seriously that this is a child who will inevitably not pass the tedious hearing screenings we do for every child in the school, on an annual basis.

We had a Middle School (11-15 years) student come to the office last week and ask to use the office desk-type phone. Now, it is a push button desk unit, has a receiver with a curly cord, and is relatively new. It is an office phone! A young lady came up to the office to call her parent, dialed the number, then turned and asked the Secretary where the "send" button was. You CANNOT make this stuff up! Another student came up to use this phone, and asked how to dial the (–) in the home phone number. Okay now, I struggle with some of the newer technology, but I think somewhere along the way we have lost a major part of our basic knowledge, along with the skills of spelling, communicating face-to-face, and social relationships. Someone show this child how to use a regular desk phone, please. She needs to call her Mother, and they cannot use their cell phones in the building......and even that is not a reality!

Hair color is another issue in middle school....and might I mention that our district does not have any dress code as to how bright or unconventional the hair color may be. I don't think any of them do these days, as everywhere I go, I see wild and crazy colors. It is very challenging, and almost comical, when having a very serious or dubious conversation with a young lady who has all the colors of the rainbow, but much less subtle or natural, in her hair. How about disciplining a young man in his behaviors and choices he is making that are not always good, who has a hairdo something like a fighting rooster, with spikes standing up for six or so inches, and colored any color you can imagine. It is just very hard to keep a straight face. My, oh my!

COMING TO THE END OF THIS STORY IS NOT EASY.....

CHAPTER 31

Okay, the stories could go on forever, but it is time to wrap it up. I have covered many aspects and experiences in my Nursing career. At some point in our lives, we Nurses must "hang up our stethoscope" and fade into the surrounding non-nursing world. I do not know quite how to do it yet, but as I approach seventy years old, it must be done.

What I look forward to are some small luxuries that I have not enjoyed for a very long time. I crave the luxury of sleeping late in the morning, watching morning news shows, wearing my pajamas until I am ready to dress, and not having a schedule to meet every day, under all kinds of circumstances. I want to plant flowers around my home, and water & nurture them. I want to go visit neighbors long neglected. I want to do lunch with my other retired friends when I want to. I want to volunteer, and if I want to stay home because it is snowing, I can. I want to dispose of my current wardrobe, wearing what I want to, not what is regulation. I want to pick up my grandchildren from school and go have ice cream, if we choose.

I want to enjoy my mornings, as well as my evenings, with my husband, who I have neglected for so many years. I want us to just have some conversations, without using him as my sounding board and emotional punching bag after a particularly tough day! He has been so willing, and appropriately silent, as he attempts to offer advice and comfort me when I am stressed. I want to try new recipes, meet new people my own age, and not wear a good basic walking shoe all day, every day, but instead, go barefoot! I want to be available for my own family when they need it, make medical appointments for myself during the day, and NOT after three in the afternoon. I want to be free to be me!

Now, what I will terribly miss is not hearing children's voices every day, and not listening to their wonderful stories and adventures. I will miss the hugs as we walk down the hallway between classes, the greetings and waves I receive from all the little people around me in school each day. I will miss seeing my best friends, my colleagues in the schools, everyday. Their hugs, I will miss, too. I will miss being their soft place to fall on tough days, their confessor, good listener, encourager, and tissue provider when times are hard. I will miss sharing my hard times with people who genuinely care, and sharing my celebrations and good times. I will miss visiting with them, laughing with them, and sharing the events of the day as they unfold around the school.

I will miss the people, because that is what Nurses are….people persons. I LOVE being with people, and I will miss that most of all! I will miss collaborating with other School Nurses struggling with the same issues we all work on every day, and celebrating victories in Nursing, when they come.

Who knows….maybe after "retiring", I will return to be a Nurse another day! The opportunity is always there! We shall see. As you likely have already figured out, I am always up for a new adventure!

Thank you for sharing this adventure with me, and if I have influenced anyone to be….or not to be….a Nurse, you must do what works for you. I will always be a Nurse, retired or not. I will never stop loving this career path I have chosen, as it has been the true joy of my life. I would not change a single thing, as I have grown and become who I am due to that career choice I made back in high school. I had no idea where it would lead me but it has been the journey of a lifetime and the joy within my soul! It has made me a better person, personally….also, a better Mother, wife, and adult woman. It has earned me the respect that Nurses deserve, and for that I am grateful and proud.

As I watch my Nursing colleagues around me retire, year after year, I have a mixture of sadness and jealousy. I vary emotionally from day to day whether I am ready to face retirement from one of the most fulfilling and satisfying careers in the world. I did have a friend tell me recently that when I no longer vary in my decision, and decide it is time to actually retire, then it IS actually time. I am not there yet, and who knows when I will get there. Right now I love what I do and I do what I love. It doesn't get any better than that!

I know I won't ever be able to work the hospital units like I did years ago…..it is too exhausting for any older Nurse. I loved teaching, but my fire for that is also out. I don't want to be known as that old cranky School Nurse who "needs to retire", so I suspect one day I will just do it. I will know. I will just retire.

Thankfully, I have truly experienced some of the most exciting aspects of Nursing, and I have no regrets. It is my identity and my spirit….that of caring for others…..What you have here is truly the reason "why on earth anyone would ever want to become a Nurse!"

Why wouldn't they? It is truly a gift to give others, and yourself, every day of your life!